# SALES
# AND
# ADVERTISEMENT MANAGEMENT



**Dr. S. RAJKUMAR**
*Research Advisor*
*P.G and Research Department of Commerce,*
*Ponnaiyah Ramajayam College,*
*Thanjavur (Distt.) - Tamil Nadu.*

**Dr. V. RAJAGOPALAN**
*Research Advisor*
*P.G. and Research Department of Commerce*
*A.V.V.M. Sri Pushpam College, (Autonomous) Poondi,*
*Thanjavur (Distt.) - Tamil Nadu.*

**S.CHAND & COMPANY LTD.**
**(AN ISO 9001 : 2000 COMPANY)**
**RAM NAGAR, NEW DELHI – 110 055**

**S. CHAND & COMPANY LTD.**
**(An ISO 9001 : 2000 Company)**
*Head Office* : 7361, RAM NAGAR, NEW DELHI - 110 055
Phones : 23672080-81-82, 9899107446, 9911310888;
Fax : 91-11-23677446
Shop at: **schandgroup.com;** E-mail: **schand@vsnl.com**

*Branches* :

- 1st Floor, Heritage, Near Gujarat Vidhyapeeth, Ashram Road, **Ahmedabad**-380 014. Ph. 27541965, 27542369, ahmedabad@schandgroup.com
- No. 6, Ahuja Chambers, 1st Cross, Kumara Krupa Road, **Bangalore**-560 001. Ph : 22268048, 22354008, bangalore@schandgroup.com
- 238-A M.P. Nagar, Zone 1, **Bhopal** - 462 011. Ph : 4274723. bhopal@schandgroup.com
- 152, Anna Salai, **Chennai**-600 002. Ph : 28460026, chennai@schandgroup.com
- S.C.O. 2419-20, First Floor, Sector- 22-C (Near Aroma Hotel), **Chandigarh**-160022, Ph-2725443, 2725446, chandigarh@schandgroup.com
- 1st Floor, Bhartia Tower, Badambadi, **Cuttack**-753 009, Ph-2332580; 2332581, cuttack@schandgroup.com
- 1st Floor, 52-A, Rajpur Road, **Dehradun**-248 001. Ph : 2740889, 2740861, dehradun@schandgroup.com
- Pan Bazar, **Guwahati**-781 001. Ph : 2738811, guwahati@schandgroup.com
- Sultan Bazar, **Hyderabad**-500 195. Ph : 24651135, 24744815, hyderabad@schandgroup.com
- Mai Hiran Gate, **Jalandhar** - 144008 . Ph. 2401630, 5000630, jalandhar@schandgroup.com
- A-14 Janta Store Shopping Complex, University Marg, Bapu Nagar, **Jaipur** - 302 015, Phone : 2719126, jaipur@schandgroup.com
- Kachapilly Square, Mullassery Canal Road, Ernakulam, **Kochi**-682 011. Ph : 2378207, cochin@schandgroup.com
- 285/J, Bipin Bihari Ganguli Street, **Kolkata**-700 012. Ph : 22367459, 22373914, kolkata@schandgroup.com
- Mahabeer Market, 25 Gwynne Road, Aminabad, **Lucknow**-226 018. Ph : 2626801, 2284815, lucknow@schandgroup.com
- Blackie House, 103/5, Walchand Hirachand Marg , Opp. G.P.O., **Mumbai**-400 001. Ph : 22690881, 22610885, mumbai@schandgroup.com
- Karnal Bag, Model Mill Chowk, Umrer Road, **Nagpur**-440 032 Ph : 2723901, 2777666 nagpur@schandgroup.com
- 104, Citicentre Ashok, Govind Mitra Road, **Patna**-800 004. Ph : 2300489, 2302100, patna@schandgroup.com
- 291/1, Ganesh Gayatri Complex, 1st Floor, Somwarpeth, Near Jain Mandir, **Pune**-411011. Ph : 64017298, pune@schandgroup.com
- Flat No. 104, Sri Draupadi Smriti Apartment, East of Jaipal Singh Stadium, Neel Ratan Street, Upper Bazar, **Ranchi**-834001. Ph: 2208761, ranchi@schandgroup.com
- Kailash Residency, Plot No. 4B, Bottle House Road, Shankar Nagar, **Raipur.** Ph. 09981200834 raipur@schandgroup.com



*First Edition 2009*

ISBN : 81-219-3067-7
Code : 07 469

PRINTED IN INDIA

*By Rajendra Ravindra Printers (Pvt.) Ltd., 7361, Ram Nagar, New Delhi-110 055 and published by S. Chand & Company Ltd., 7361, Ram Nagar, New Delhi-110 055.*

*Dedicated to*

*Our Family Members*

# FOREWORD

A sale is a vast subject but it is an inevitable part of functioning of every society. In this book, the authors have enumerated the basic principles of sales management and elucidated them keeping in view the needs of the undergraduate and postgraduate students of Commerce and Management Studies of various universities. . The treatment of the theme of "Sales Management" is illuminating and logical because of the rich experience of the teachers in corporate field and in teaching college students for more than two decades. Beyond any shadow of doubt the book will help students score high marks in the university examinations.

The authors have presented the basics of sales and its latest dimensions by focusing on advertising and its impact in the minds of the modern men.

I confidently opine that this book and the efforts of the authors will prove to be successful and beneficial to the students.

**Dr. S. SEKAR,**
M.Com. M.B.A., M.Phil., Ph.D.,
Reader and Head,
P.G. and Research Department of Commerce,
Urumu Dhanalakshmi College,
Kattur, Tiruchirappalli – 620 019,
Tamil Nadu, South India.

# PREFACE

The basics and scope of sales management is of critical importance. The role and various aspects of sales are dealt with in a lucid and logical manner. The cause and effect relationship between advertising and sales is highlighted and the advertising is analyzed in all its important aspects. This book which will prove to be handy to learn the starting and promotion of sales with the help of advertising to maximize profit is essential for the undergraduate and post graduate students of Commerce and Management Studies of various universities. This book on **"Sales and Advertisement Management"** gives a simple and clear knowledge of an efficient implementation and management of sales by narrating the basics and its scope in this competitive world

We thank Mrs. Nirmala Gupta, Managing Director, M/s. S.Chand & Co., New Delhi for his patronizing support in the publications of this book. Mr. Navin Joshi, Vice President (Publishing) has helped us a lot in the early execution of this work. Mr.R.S.Saxena, Advisor, Publications Division of S.Chand & Co helped us a lot to transform our thoughts into books in your hands. Mr.A.M.Arunachalam, Manager, Chennai Branch and Mr.R.K.K.Swamy, Assistant Manager, Chennai Branch bulldozed the practical difficulties and ensured a smooth completion of this work.

We are extremely greatful and thankful to Kalvikavalar Sriman K.Thulasiah Vandayar, Correspondent, A.V.V.M. Sri Pushpam College, (Autonomous), Poondi, Thanjavur District and Kalvi Vallal Prof. Pon. Murugesan, Chancellor, PRIST University, Thanjavur, Tamil Nadu for their kind whole hearted support extended in bringing out this edition successfully.

Through out the period of preparation of the manuscripts, our morale was kept high by the unstained support and encouragement provided by Dr. S. Sekar, Reader and Head, P.G. and Research Department of Commerce, Urumu Dhanalakshmi College, Tiruchirappalli. We remain indebted to these scholars and executives for their valuable guidance and cooperation.

Suggestions, advice, comments, criticisms etc., from readers, are most welcome and will be made use of in the next edition.

**Dr. S. Rajkumar**

**Dr. V. Rajagopalan**

# CONTENTS

## SALES MANAGEMENT



## ADVERTISING MANAGEMENT

# Sales Management

# 1 Sales Management

## MEANING :

Sales management is the successful management of company sales or sales activities? It is with direction and control of sales. Therefore sales planning, co-ordination of marketing research, advertising and sales promotion on the other hand merchandising and integration of all business activities which contribute to the increased sales and profit are done through marketing programmes. Thus it is to manage sales activities and functions and sales army who are the backbone of sales department occupying activities and sub activities.

## OBJECTIVES OF SALES MANAGEMENT

The basic objectives of sales management are three, namely

### 1. Sales maximization

Sales Maximisation is not an easy task. Maximisation of sales implies increase in the quantity of goods sold and therefore, increase in Sales volume. For a new concern, it is to start from scratch having no past experience. Most of the newly started companies follow the leaders in the line and their competitors and the detailed study of strength, weakness, opportunities and threats. Most of the companies have failed because they have not been able to sell what they could produce. A successful company is one, which understands the consumer in entirely his specifications and makes available goods and services accordingly in terms of product, price, quantity, quality, right time and proper promotion. Once they make debt, then demand can be increased and maintained. In the case of existing companies the problems of increasing sales are quite different. They are known in the market and hence they try to hunt virgin markets say moving from district level market to state level from state level to national level and from national level to international level.

### 2. Profit maximization

One might think and say that profit maximization is not a difficult task. If sales are increased profit will automatically increase. A sound firm is not interested only in profit minimization but improvement in profitability rate. It should be noted that profit and profitability are two different concepts though they are closely related. Profit might increase in absolute terms but might not be commensurate with the efforts put in. Profitability improvement definitely leads to increase imports and not otherwise true necessarily.

### 3. Attainment of continued growth

This objective is of topmost importance. Sales maximization and profit maximization can be attained with comparatively easy and cost efforts. However, achieving continued growth is some thing challenging and thrilling and rewarding. Like product each organization has a life cycle namely birth, growth, expansion, maturity and decline. Most of the firms struggle hard to grow and expand and reach the peak height of performance. However once they reach the peak of prosperity or maturity, they do not stay longer in that span of life cycle.

## SCOPE AND NATURE OF SALES MANAGEMENT

Today department of sales is a sub-system of a system. It is responsible for creating, maintaining and extending the class of customers. Any firm that creates and maximizes this asset has no fear of fall. Any firm, which is not consumer in its approach, fails. In the question of profit maximizations any firm can think of ignoring consumer satisfaction and maximum social advantage. Thus, the very sour failure of any organization is largely hinged on sales management or sales department contribution is the total achievement of organization as a whole. In view of its significant contribution, it has to care for sales activities, advertising and publicity, sales promotions and public relations as internal actions, a sound relation with other departments of the organization.

## FUNCTIONS OF SALES MANAGEMENT

Sales Management is a highly functional and specialized aspect of management. Its functions range from pre-sales and post-sales activities. In order to achieve the basic or fundamental objective, practically it does all the functions of general management as applied to this area of sales, namely:

- Planning
- Organizing
- Directing
- Coordinating
- Motivating and
- Controlling

The sales manager like a general manager has to perform all those functions of getting the work done ranging from planning to control as far as his field is concerned. The functions of sales management mean the functions of a sales manager; He is the head or the brain behind the army of sales force and their superiors who work under him. The functions are

1. Sales Planning
2. Sales Organizing
3. Sales Directing
4. Sales Co-Coordinating
5. Sales Motivating
6. Sales controlling

### 1. Sales Planning

Planning is the process of thinking before doing. It works on the basis of the statement. ***"Look before you leap"***. It is to do with determining the future course of action.

Prof. H.Koontz, *"Planning is an intellectual process, the conscious determination of course of action, the basis of decisions as purpose, facts and considered estimates."*

**The Sales Manager has to attain three basic goals namely**

1. Increasing the sales contributing more and more to profits
2. Creating consumer demand.
3. Maintaining the continuous growth

Every Sales Manager is responsible for sales objectives and determining the sales and advertising activities and sales promotion activities that is essential to attain the pre-established goals.

Sales planning involve the coordinating activities of salesman, dealers and advertising, physical distribution, production. Scheduling, inventories, budgeting, advertising and Sales efforts.

As a successful planner, he is to analyze different elements or components of sales-with the assistance of his trustworthy subordinates – such as.

- Personal Selling
- Sales Promotion techniques
- Advertising and Publicities
- Sales budgets
- Markets and their Segments
- Consumer behaviour and
- Psychology

This will help in setting sales – quotas and sales territories for performance and performance evaluation of his sales force. Such an attempt keeps him in setting goals by salesman take periodwise, area wise, cost wise. Sales manager being the head, he should do this wonderful for his subordinates support.

Thus, Sales planning en-compasses variant aspects as Sales objectives and goals, sales policies, procedures and programmes, sales budget, sales strategies in the short-and long-term sales management.

## Setting Objectives

The first and foremost function of Sales planning is to determine the Sales objectives. Without any objective, the firm will not achieve their target or goals.

**(*a*) Forecasting**

Sales objective and sales process, quality designs of the product are total market and each market basis of records of past years. They collect all the informations bearing on the customers, competition, potential markets, and products and so on.

**(*b*) Budgeting**

If refers to inflows and outflows of resources estimated by planners. The sales budget refers to the volume of sales to be achieved during a particular period Viz. month, year.

**(*c*) Strategy**

The sales manager decides the strategy in light of the suggestions made by sales representation and on the recommendations of the top level management. How to approach the buyer and organize a sales group? Technical salesman may approach customers before, during and after the sales.

**(*d*) Programming**

These are the specific activities to be performed by workers in future. Each salesman decides how to achieve the pre-determined objectives.

**2. Sales Organizing**

Sales planning are the first step in the sales management. The sales plan and its projective cannot be realized unless he goes ahead with sales organization.

The term organization has two distinct meanings. As a structure, it is the network of horizontal and vertical dimensions designed to attain definite common goals. It is the mechanism or the framework of the past whereby people, functions and facilities are integrated to achieve the present goals.

In that it is the function of identifying grouping the work to be performed defining and delegating the responsibilities and empowering so that the given job's can be performed effectively, and economically.

A successful sales manager is one who knows the art of organizing that creates an atmosphere where subordinates are ready and willing to contribute their best. It is possible by creating work atmosphere and work-culture.

The manager divides his sales department into sub-departments and sections. His sales department becomes a sales organization, an organization within the overall organization.

The most common sub-departments or sections of sales department are marketing research, advertising, sales – promotion, personnel which are further divided into selection, training and employee relations. In addition he is to have packing and shipping departments.

**3. Sales Directing**

As a leader, the sales manager is to direct his subordinates towards the attainment of selling objectives. Directing as a function of management has three basic ingredients namely.

(*a*) Issuing orders and instructions for the best possible performance of various activities so assigned.

(*b*) Guiding, teaching, coaching and making his subordinates worthy of developing self confidence of doing their work even in his absence and

(*c*) Supervising the subordinates to ensure that their performance confirms to the standards laid down in the sales plan for the coming period.

As a leader, Sales Manager is expected to take initiative to represent his enterprise, to administer the department, to interpret the changes and to encourage the team-work.

**4. Sales Coordinating**

Activity is the outcome of group or a team. To convert consumer desires into goods and services and back them to sales giving satisfaction to the customers and profits to the organization.

A well co-ordinated enterprise is one where each department, division, section and finally each services and back them to sales giving satisfaction to the customers and profits to the organization.

It is are orderly arrangement of group efforts to provide unity of thought, purpose and action. It is a matter of integrating the efforts, timing the operations and balancing the conflicting interests.

**5. Sales motivation**

Motivation of people in the organization is a constructive force and a core of management process. In fact motivation is another side of direction and leadership. It is the psychological technique of executing the plan. Policies and programmes through the efforts of others.

The Sales Manager is to design a sound remuneration plan which is attractive rewarding those reducing sales cost, sticking the employers to the organization, Homely and patient. A good remuneration plan attracts good employees rewards the efficient and punishes the inefficient, serves as a motivating force and keeps the employees tied to the organization as loyal employees. These plans of remuneration can be purely salary based; straight commission based coordination of commission and salary, salary commission and bonus based.

Sales motivation is known for improving employees efficiency, relieving them from tension keeping Sales force happy and instilling a human treatment. For, the sales manager is to develop and use the tools of motivation, such as personal contact. Personnel manager is expected to recruit the candidates for the posts of salesman select them, train them, place them, equip them, direct them, co-ordinate their energies and efforts, motivate them to the best of their abilities and control them with the frame work of set targets and constraints to make functions more flexible and working. There may be sub-departments and sections. The actual success depends on sales force, its strength and quality.

**6. Sales Controlling**

The sales manager has to control the sales activities of the sub ordinates, as he is accountable to his higher authorities. Control is the task of regularity in the employee work performance in line with the pre-determined plans to ensure the attainment of organizational goals. Control function consists of verifying whether everything is occurring in conformity with the plan. It is the measurement of performance against the promise and finding out the extent of the causes of gaps between what is promised and performed, so that corrective action might be taken if need then be.

To achieve selling objective, the sales manager is to control variants of personal selling efforts to ensure the attainment of pre-self objective with no or little waste. It means, that is a question of target setting in terms of sales quotas and sales-territories, output and inputs, comparing actual performance with these planned high-lights, finding out the extent and causes of variance – may be favourable or unfavourable and taking corrective action to set the derailment back to normalcy. It is basically evaluation preceded by analysis and followed by interpretation. His analysis – spotlights on sales results – marketing costs – area wise, product wise, time wise, customer wise and salesman wise – individual performance or efficiency rate in focus, advertising programmes and their impact on sales improvement, performance of different middlemen in terms of their knowledge about consumers and their behaviour. This helps the sales management to make vital decisions on products, policies, profit, promotion, wage and salary administration, inventory management, public relations and so on.

## REVIEW QUESTIONS

1. What do you mean by Sales Management?
2. State the basic objectives of Sales Management.
3. State the basic goals to be attained by a Sales Manager.
4. What do you mean by Sales Planning?
5. What do you mean by Sales Control?
6. Explain the nature and Scope of Sales Management.
7. Briefly explain the various functions of Sales Management.

# 2 Sales Policy

## MEANING AND DEFINITION OF SALES POLICY

The success of sales organization in any business enterprise depends on its sales policy. Hence the business enterprise should formulate its sales policy before starting sales. A sales policy is a settled on long-term course of procedure affecting sales. The establishment, direction and control of sales organization is done on the basis of sales policy. Some of the main definitions of sales policy are as follows:

1. According to Harold Whitehead, *"A sales policy is laid down as the basis and for the guidance of the selling operations of a business."*
2. According to J.S.K. Patel, *"A sales policy is a settled or definite long-term course of procedure affecting sales"*.
3. According to Still and Cundiff, *"Sales policies are the guidelines set up by management within which the company is to seek to reach its personal selling objectives."*

Generally the sales policy is not permanent. It has to be changed from time to time according to circumstances. A sales manager formulates different sales plans and controls different sales efforts on the basis of sales policy. But the responsibility of implementing sales policy virtually lies on the sales manager. In some business enterprises sales policy is formulated by the sales manager but it is sent for approval to the top level management.

## NEED FOR FORMULATING SALES POLICY

1. It enables the sales manager to act promptly along well-considered line of action.
2. It enables the sales force to take decision in time. Further uniformity of action is ensured in all fields.
3. Sales policy is essential for directing and controlling the activities of the sales force.
4. Sales policies are in respect of changing business conditions and hence ensure adoption of sound methods to secure sales and profits.
5. Sales policy is essential for the future development of business. All the future sales plans are based on sales policy.
6. According to Harold Whitehead, "the sales policy regulates the relationship between the business and distributions to the public".
7. Sales policy is needed for providing necessary information to dealers, distributors, salesmen consumers and sales managers etc. such as, terms and conditions of sale, terms of providing credit and policy as to price discounts etc.
8. Sales policy is needed for providing satisfaction to buyers and consumers, such as after-sales service, sale on approval and money refund guarantee etc.,

## THE PRINCIPLES OF FORMULATION OF SALES POLICY.

Like other policies, sales policy should also be based on some principles. The main principles of the formulation of sales policy are as follows:

### 1. Principle of Competition

Competition in the same line of trade has a direct impact on the sales policy. Hence the sales policy should be formulated on the basis of the competition that exists in the trade. Unless the product has something plus as against the competitive product, it cannot be sold easily, Consumer's goodwill is the soul of the sales policy and it can be established only when the product is in a position to face the competition effectively. For creating consumer's goodwill, it is essential that the produce should be standardized and suitable consumer's services are also provided, such as, after-sale service, repair service, exchange facility and sale on return etc. For instance, Hindustan Lever Limited, Mumbai pays much attention on providing consumer's services besides manufacturing standardized products and thus occupy key position in the market.

### 2. Principle of Pricing

Principle of pricing plays an important role in formulating sales policy. While fixing the price of the product, the manufacturer or the producer should not be concerned only with protecting his own intention consider that of the consumers. He should see that the price policy adopted by the company helps to expand his business. The price should be fair – neither too low nor too high.

### 3. Principle of Extent of the Market

The extent of the market of the product is also an important principle, which should be kept in mind while formulating the sales policy. If the area of the market is small, then the sales organization will adopt intensive sales policy. On the contrary, if the area of the market is large, then the sales organization will adopt extensive sales policy.

### 4. Nature of the Product

Nature of the product is an important factor or principle which should be kept in mind while formulating sales policy of a company. The market may consist of different types of customers belonging to the higher class, the higher-middle class, the middle class and the lower class. If the product is meant for lower-class people then it can command a wide market provided it is quite cheaper as compared to competitor's product. The policy should be formulated accordingly.

### 5. Scale of Production

The scale of production may be small or large. If the scale of production is large then the cost of production per unit will be quite low and thus the sales force may cover wide market. The company will also earn handsome profits. On the contrary, if the scale of production is small then the cost of product per unit will be quite high and hence the sales force can cover small or limited market only. The overall profit will also be quite low. Hence this factor should also be kept in mind while formulating sales policy.

## REVIEW QUESTIONS

1. What is a Sales Policy?
2. Who forms a Sales Policy?
3. Why a Sales Policy should be framed?
4. Explain the need for formulating a Sales Policy.
5. Explain the Principles for formulation of Sales Policy

# 3 Sales Organization

## SALES ORGANIZATION

Sales Organization is the part of the overall organization structure. It is one that establishes coordination among various sales functions, necessary for the achievement of sales and overall corporate goals. It is the framework of relations wherein the functions related with profitable sales are carefully and consciously planned and coordinated as to place all the products of the firm in the hands of final users. Thus, it is the structural segment of a business organization which is designed and integrated so that the efforts of the persons can be coordinated for attaining the best results-economic and social for individuals and groups.

## SIGNIFICANCE OF SALES ORGANIZATION

The importance of sales organization can be seen in the following points. That is a sales organization is a must because of the following reasons.

1. To plan purchases
2. To create a pattern of demand for products
3. To handle the orders received
4. To collect the clues
5. To reconcile the complaints
6. To handle the tasks of personnel management

### 1. To Plan Purchase

The firm's sales are depending on the state of prospects of it. That is, firm will sell those products and service, which are needed by the people. Consumer is the 'big-boss' who decide the dimensions of what he wants, where he wants, when he wants, at what cost he wants, of what quality he wants and so on.

This big-boss is the king pin and the firm will have to develop product planning and development accordingly. To plan the purchase or fabrication in terms of different assortments a viable organization is a must, It is already noted that the salesman is the buying agent of a customer.

### 2. To create a pattern of demand for products

The products of the firm are not sold themselves. Somebody must be there to push from the shelves to the bags of consumer. Such push is not physical one, it is psychological. Salesman does it directly and advertising indirectly. After all, advertising is not a divine power but a brainchild of human beings. The personnel convincing people directly or indirectly are the integral part of sales organization.

**3. To handle the orders received**

Selling routine calls for highly specialized tasks of receiving enquires entertaining them with latest and least quotations, appearing for orders, receiving orders, packing the products as per the instructions of the customers, preparing invoice, despatching them to the expectations of the buyers – may be individuals or the organizations.

**4. To collect the dues**

Credit sales form the bulk share in these days of fast moving world of competition, is a must. If one speaks only of hard cash business, the sales organization has to pull the shutters down because; credit is the breath of economic transactions. Credit sales warrant is to be handled with care, because, the selling house is to collect the dues but keep the customers as they are finally referred as "the making laws". Collection of dues is like performing a tight-rope dance where almost care is to be taken to maintain the balance which is the secret of success.

**5. To reconcile the complaints**

Complaints are common in these days where customers are more and more aware of their rights and conscious of what they pay for the products. Their complaints are to be heard, analyzed and are to be settled. It is of special importance because; the firm is to have good public relations. The attitude towards customers should be *'Customers are always right'*.

**6. To handle the tasks of personnel Management**

Management of sales force demands well in many activities. Sales-force is to be selected trained, placed, transferred, promoted, motivated, maintained and controlled by the superiors. Each aspect of manpower development and maintenance is bold and challenging one. The terms of talent, time and treasure is required as investment.

## TYPES OF SALES ORGANIZATION

Organization is an entity designed to identify and group the work to be performed, defining and delegating the authorities and responsibilities and establishing relationships to enable the people within the organization to work with efficiency and effectively towards the attainment of the general and specific goals.

**1. Physical Distribution Department**

*'Physical Distribution'* encompasses the functions of storage, packing despatching and transportation. The subordinates responsible for handling these specialized activities assist the person in charge. Storage section cares for designing better ways and means of storage to care for the goods from the time they check in and till they checkout.

Packing section works hard to meet the requirements of consumers by caring for acceptable economical packaging.

Despatching section arranges for the requisitions sent by different branches of the selling organization.

Transportation section responsibilities are moving the products from factories to warehouses from warehouses to the branches and from branches to the consumers in some cases.

**2. Publicity and Sales – Promotion Department**

Advertising department plays a constructive role as a bridge between production and distribution activities of the organization. Advertising is to make known the people about the existence of goods and educate them about special features, advantages and benefits.

Advertising manager is to plan advertising programme, budget, and select media and implement the programs and strategies. Generally, this advertising task namely planning and placing is handed over to specialized service namely advertising agencies.

Advertising Manager is also responsible for sales – promotion. It is a system of efforts designed to improve the sales by focusing the attention of the consumers at the actual points of sales. It entails the tasks of display, supply of sales conference, granting attractive terms of trade, motivating dealer and consumers through contests and so on.

**3. Public Relations Department**

Public relations or the opinions about the selling house are of vital importance. Sound public relations rest upon sound policies and socially responsible behaviour. Maintenance of good contacts with the public such as customers, dealers, Government, officials, employees and other organizations.

Public relations officers are charged with the responsibilities of knowing what opinion public forms about the firm. Good public relations are to be created and maintained even at a high cost.

**4. Personnel Department**

Personnel management process which, devotes itself to the solution of all the problems that are grounded primarily on the human element in the organization. Manpower development is the main responsibility of this department

**Functions of Sales Manager**

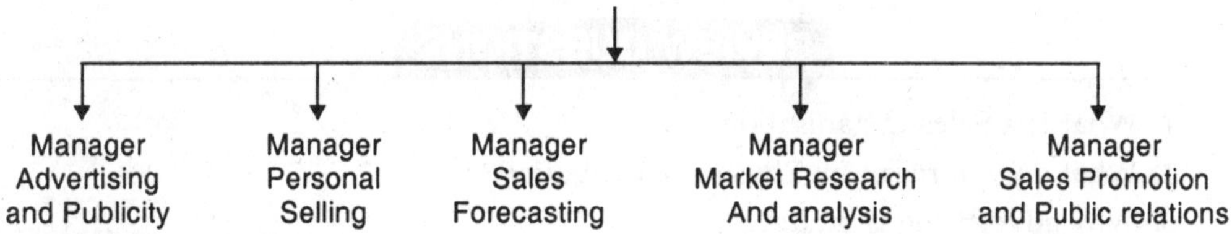


**2. Product Type**

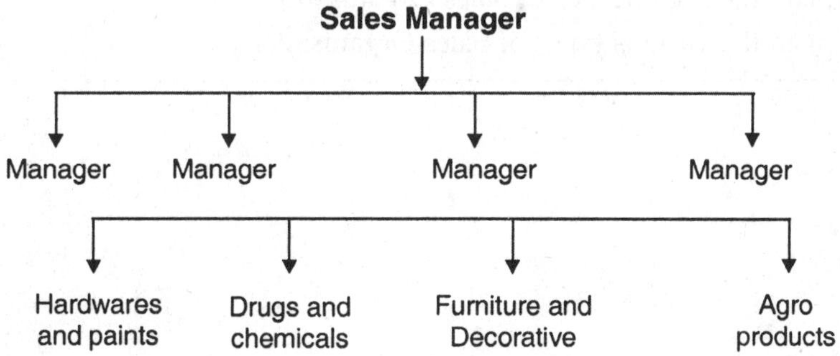


**5. Sales Department**

It is considered to be the heart of sales organization. It is the controlling nerve center. Sales Manager who is assisted by sales supervisors, salesman and sales – clerks to discharge those duties that are indispensable to execute the work of selling, heads it. The sale Manager plans travelling programme of salesmen, appoints agents give instructions to the Salesman. Thus, he does all the functions of selling routing consisting of attending the letters of enquiry, receiving orders, preparing bills and invoice, despatching goods, coordinating, motivating and controlling the efforts of his men and women in the department.

### 6. Statistics and Records Department

A modern Sales organization gets information regarding the quality of goods liked by the consumers, quantity demanded and the time when such goods are demanded by the consumers through market-research. Statistical department plays a constructive role as it collects and analyses the data so collected. Sales statistics are vital in the decision – making process that give all-round studies and factual information about products, people and policies. The record section does the work of preserving the documents and papers for future forecasting and legal evidence as a proof.

### 7. Credit and collection Department

Credit is the breath of modern business and soul of selling efforts. Credit transactions are accounting for a lion's share of total business transacted. It is the Sales executive that decides the credit and collection policies and strategies. A moderate policy of credit is desirable as it will not reduce the volume of sales on one hand and increase the bad debts on the other. If a strict and stringent policy is enforced, it may be too conservative and results in restricted sales finally reducing the profits too. On the other hand, a liberal credit policy is sure to increase the sales with likely increase in the close of bad debts.

Heavy bad debts eat away increased profits. Equally important is the crucial task of collecting the dues. Collecting policy is to be such that dues are to be collected yet the customer is to be retained. Any body can collect dues but retaining the customer loyal to the firm is really a challenging one.

## REVIEW QUESTIONS

1. What is a Sales Organisation?
2. What do you mean by Physical Distribution?
3. Why advertising is made?
4. State the functions of Sales Organisation
5. Explain the Significance of Sales Organisation
6. Explain the various types of Sales Organisations

# 4 Sales Fields or Territories

## MEANING AND DEFINITIONS OF SALES TERRITORY

A sales territory is the economic unit which is used in the planning and controlling of sales efforts. It is the division of the individual salesman for performing sales activities. Many sales executives refer to sales territory as a geographical area, which is assigned to an individual sales person for serving the customers and prospects residing in that area. According to Still, Gundiff and Govoni, *"Operationally a sales territory is a particular grouping of customers and prospects assigned to an individual sales person". According to Marry and Davis, "Sales territory is a basic unit of sales planning territory, is grouping of customers and prospects assigned to an individual salesman".*

## OBJECTIVES OR REASONS OF ESTABLISHING OR REVISING SALES TERRITORIES

The main objective or reason of establishing or revising a sales territory is to plan and control sales so as to maximize sales and profits by improving customer services and reducing selling expense ratios. Distribution of work-load among sales persons becomes easy and manageable. It is the key objective of an efficient distribution system. According to *Still Cundiff and Govani* the following are the main objectives or reasons of establishing or revising sales territories.

### 1. To Improve Market Coverage.

One of the main reasons of establishing sales territories is to improve market coverage. In the absence of proper market coverage the enterprise may lose its business to competitiors that have wide coverage and are in a position to utilize sales opportunities effectively. If sales territories are designed intelligently and assigned to sales personnel carefully, it is possible to have wide and better market coverage.

Thus in establishing sales territories the following considerations should be kept in mind

(*i*) The market is being expanded.

(*ii*) The maximum area is represented by the sales force.

(*iii*) It should permit the sales force to cover the assigned sales territories conveniently, efficiently and economically.

(*iv*) The territories should represent reasonable work-load to sales force to facilitate them to contact potential customers and prospects.

(*v*) The allocation of sales territories amongst the sales force is done according to the capacity and capability of the individual salesman.

**2. Reducing Selling Expense Ratios**

The establishment of sales territories should assist in reducing selling expense ratios. Proper routing and scheduling should minimize the visits of sales force. The proportional selling expenses should be changed as and when required. The concern of the sales management should not only be to reduce total selling expenses but to maintain proper relationship between selling expenses and sales volume. For instance, in some cases it might be possible even to increase selling expenses so as to get larger sales volume.

**3. To Improve the Customer Service**

The object of establishing sales territory is to improve the customer service. The sales territories should be designed in such a way that the salesman is in a position to provide efficient customer service and thereby providing maximum satisfaction to the customers within this assigned sales territory. The salesman should be in a position to establish regular contacts with his customers and prospects and to understand and get them solved. Improved customer services establish improved business and personal relations between the respective salesman and the customer and also raise the general reputation of the enterprise, which the salesman represents.

**4. To Improve Sales Force Interest and Morale**

The object of establishing sales territories is also to improve sales force interest and morale. Good sales territorial design helps in stimulating the interest of the sales force in their respective jobs and in increasing their morale.

Hence while designing sales territories the following factors should be kept in mind –

(*i*) the salesman is in a position to achieve the desired target conveniently.

(*ii*) The workload assigned to a salesman should be reasonable in view of his capacity and capability.

(*iii*) The respective salesmen should be aware of their responsibilities of achieving what management expects from them within their own territories. The above factors help in promoting sales force interest and morale that puts the individual salesman to hard work and also to make each salesman as productive as possible. It will also raise the self-confidence and job satisfaction among the salesmen.

**5. To Coordinate Personal Selling and Advertising Efforts**

Another objective of establishing sales territories is to establish effective coordination between personal selling and advertising. Coordination between personal selling efforts and advertising efforts is necessary for performing the selling task more efficiently and conveniently. For this purpose the size of the sales territories assigned to individual advertising campaign for a new consumer product the salesman may call upon dealers to outline the marketing plant's objectives and provide them display and other promotional materials. Thereafter he should organize his personal sales efforts in close coordination with advertising efforts. This may result in more satisfactory performance.

**6. To Improve Sales Force Performance Evaluation**

The objective of establishing sales territories is also to improve sales force performance evaluation. It is possible to have correct information about sales force through organized sales territories. The problems of territory/region to territory/region differ and thereby the efforts of solving these problems too differ accordingly. In view of this factor evaluation of sales personnel is essential and which is possible through establishing effective and convenient sales territories in accordance with the capacity and capability of the individual salesman.

**7. Meeting the Competition**

By establishing sales territories the enterprise can face the competition from competitors more effectively. When the total market is divided into different territories, the market experts may analyze a deep study. On the basis of this analysis the management may adjust and revise the selling strategies and marketing plans accordingly to meet the competition in different territories.

**8. To Increase Profitability of Sales**

By establishing sales territories the area of the market along with volume of business is increased considerably. Further, the selling expense ratio is also reduced. All this leads to an increase in the profitability of sales.

**9. To Improve Sale Planning**

By establishing sales territories there is an improvement in sales planning because of proper sales budgeting market research, sales forecasting, sales profitability analysis and the implementation of sales strategies.

**10. To Improve Control on Sales Force**

By establishing sales territories the control on sales force can be improved considerably. When the market is divided in to different sales territories, the performance of each salesman can be measured and judged both by the salesman himself and the management. On this basis, the management is in a position to have better control on sales force.

## FACTORS AFFECTING THE SALES TERRITORY

The following factors affect or determine the establishment of sales territories:

**(1) Size of Business:**

Size of business is a major factor in establishing sales territories. In case of large size business we will require a bigger sales force along with a large number of sales territories of smaller size.

**(2) Methods of Distribution:**

Methods of distribution also affect the establishment of sales territories. The enterprise may sell the products either directly to the consumers by establishing its own shops or through the chain of wholesalers and retailers.

**(3) Ability of the Salesman**

The ability of salesmen also affect the establishment of sales territories .If the enterprise is having a team of experienced and efficient salesmen, then the size of the sales territory would be comparatively large. On the contrary, if the salesmen are absolutely fresh without any experience on their credit then the size of the sales territory would be quite small.

**(4) Level of Competition**

Level of competition also affects the establishment of sales territories. In case of keen and cut-throat competition, the salesmen are expected to remain more alert and perform their duties more carefully and effectively. At such places the size of the sales territory would be comparatively small. On the contrary, where no competition exists the salesman is in a position to cover larger area and thus the size of the sales territory would be large.

**5. Means of Advertisement and Sales Promotion**

Means of advertisement and sales promotion also affect the establishment of sales territories. When the enterprise is using various means of advertisement and sales promotion on a wide scale, the size of the sales territory would be large. On the contrary, if the enterprise is not using the various means of advertisement and sales promotion, the size of the sales territory would be quite small.

**6. Density of Population**

Density of population also affects the establishment of sales territories. If the area is thickly populated, people residing in that area have better chances of augmenting their income like Delhi, Mumbai, Calcutta, Chennai, Punjab, Haryana and U.P. etc. In this case, the size of sales territory would be small. Augmenting one's income are less in places such as Assam, Rajasthan and M.P. The size of sales territory would be large.

**7. Market Potentialities**

Market potentialities also affect the size of sales territory. If the market has vast sales potentialities (such as Calcutta, Chennai, Mumbai, Jaipur, Indore etc.) then it would have a small sales territory. On the contrary, if the market possesses less sales potentialities then it would have a larger sales territory.

**8. Demand of the Product**

Demand of the product is also an important factor of determining the size of a sales territory. If the demand of the product is quite high (such as Tata Salt, Lux Soap, Hero Cycle, etc.) the size of the sales territory would be quite small. On the contrary If the demand of the product is quite low, the size of the sales territory would be comparatively quite large.

**9. Transport Facilities**

Transport facilities also affect the size of the sales territory. The areas which are served with good means of transport and communications have better chances of expansion of trade and thus will have a small sales territory .On the contrary, transport bottlenecks are responsible for the stagnation of trade and thereby there will be a larger sales territory.

**10. Cost of sales territory**

Cost of sales territory also affects the size of sales territory. If the cost of sales territory is high, i.e. Expenses of sales are high as compared to sales in a sales territory; it would have large sales territory. On the contrary, if the cost of sales territory is low, i.e., the expenses of sales are low as compared to sales in a sales territory, it would have comparatively a small sales territory.

**11. Policy of the Enterprise.**

Policy of the enterprise affects the size of the sales territory. If the policy of the enterprise is to have large scale production, less profit, low price level and maximum sales, the size of the sales territory would be a small one. On the contrary, if the policy of the enterprise is to have small production, high prices and maximization of profits, the size of the sales territory would be comparatively quite large.

**Consideration should be kept in mind in allocation of sales territory**

The allocation of sales territories arises only after determining sales territories. The allocation of sales territories is an important function of the sales manager. It should be done after due thinking and in a planned way. The sales manager must also demonstrate that he is quite impartial to all the salesmen under his control and he is that equally humanitarian in his approach. According to Gauss, Whiteman and Bates, the sales manager must bear the following points in mind while allocating sales territories :

(1) Every possible effort should be made to prevent duplication of efforts. Two salesmen may not be allotted the same territory.

(2) While allocating sales territories it should be kept in mind that as far as possible sales opportunities are equaly divided. There must be no discrimination in this respect.

(3) The allocation of sales territories should be done in such a way that it may facilitate the effective control of the sales manager on the sales force and develop healthy competition amongst the salesmen.

(4) Allocation of sales territories should facilitate comparison among the Sales personnel.

(5) Allocation of sales territories should provide for proper and efficient routing of salesman. Every salesman should be in a position to perform his daily routine efficiently. All the work to be attended to in one round must be planned in advance.

(6) Allocation of sales territories should avoid wastage and facilitate economy. The selling cost should suit the amount of sales.

(7) Allocation of sales territories should provide flexibility so that the changes may be done conveniently without disturbing the structure; etc.

(8) Allocation of sales territory should be done in such a way that it may provide equality of income to salesmen. Allocation of territories should not be based on the basis of geographical areas alone because these may be vast areas without any scope of sales (such as Assam) while many small areas (such as Calcutta, Mumbai, Chennai, Jaipur etc.) may have a large scope of sales. Hence allocation of territories should be made on the basis of sales. It would ensure equal earning possibilities.

(9) Allocation of sales territories should provide even coverage. The sales territory allocated to a salesman should be neither too small nor too big; it should be such that it can be easily handled by a salesman.

(10) Equitable assignment should be done. It should be based on the competence, skill, ability, experience and the knowledge of the salesmen. If the circumstances in a particular territory demand the presence of particular salesman of requisite ability or influence he should be given that territory in spite of the claims of other salesmen.

(11) Allocation of sales territories should be done on the basis of demand of the product and the elasticity of demand so that the advantages of discriminating price policy can accrue.

(12) New salesmen should not be given independent charge of a sales territory at the first instance. He should be required to work under the direct supervision and control of experienced salesmen for some time.

## METHODS OF ESTABLISHING THE SALES TERRITORIES

There are different methods of establishing sales territories. For instance, sales territories may be established on the basis of the size of business unit, nature of the product, the number of consumers to be reached, extent of competition, services rendered towards the customers and their purchasing capacity and the structure of the organization or the enterprise etc. If sales territories are established on the basis of above factors they will be ideal and on scientific lines and it can help a lot in commanding good sales. In this age of keen competition different methods are used for establishing sales territories. The main methods used for establishing sales territories are as follows:

(1) **On the Basis of country Unit:** When the sale of a product is done on international level (such as petrol, tea and coffee etc.) then the whole country is treated as one unit and thus only one sales territory is established for the whole country. Indian Tea Board had established one sales territory in our country.

(2) **On the Basis of state unit**: Under this method sales territories are established on state or province basis. Once sales territory is established for the entire state or province, the same sales territory is responsible for selling the product of an enterprise in that particular state. Several Indian industries are on state basis.

(3) **On the Basis of District Unit**: Under this method sales territories are established on the basis of district. Under this method one sales territory is established for one district. For instance, Usha Sewing Machine, Asian Paints, Tata Soap etc. have established sales territory on the basis of the district, i.e. one sales territory for each district. This method is adopted when there is a wide market for the product and the number of customer is quite large.

(4) **Other Methods**: Besides the above methods, sales territories can also be established on regional basis, size of production, unit basis etc.

**The various steps in the procedures for setting up new sales territories or revising the existing sales territories.**

There are different steps in the procedures for setting up new sales territories or revising the existing sales territories. The main steps involved are as follows:

### (1) Selecting a Basic Geography Control Unit

The first step involved in the procedures for setting up new sales territories or revising the existing sales territories is selecting a basic geographical districts, zones or states or trading areas. Sales territories are put together as consolidation of basic geographical control units. The control unit should be a small one. The choice of the control units, i.e. cities, districts, zones on states or trading areas depends on the statistical data available in government records. In this case the enterprise has nothing to spend on collection of information for the sales territory. In this way it becomes easy and less expensive to develop the requisite market and sales potential. On the contrary, if no statistical data are available on such geographical control unit, the enterprise will have to spend a lot of money on collection and analyzing information in respect of such control units.

### 2. Determining Sales Potential in Control Unit

The second step involved in the procedure for setting up new sales territories or revising the existing sales territories is to determine the sales potential present in each control unit so that the territorial planners may estimate the sales potential representing the maximum sales opportunities present in that control unit for the products in a given period in particular market segments or geographical control units. The territorial planners identify buyers of the product. The identification of buyers should be precisely descriptive for a control unit. Formal market identification should be conducted by marketing research personnel to make them more reliable. After identifying the potential buyers the territorial planners should determine the sales potential for the product in each control unit.

### 3. Combining Control Units into Tentative Sales Territories

This is, the third step involved in the procedures for setting up new sales territories or revising the existing sales territories Here the planner has to determine only tentative sales territory without making any adjustment for converge difficulty and assuming that each such control unit has no major differences in the physical or other characteristics. It contains approximately the same sales potential. Now the next question arises about purpose. The planner, taking all the sales personnel to be of average ability, should estimate the percentage of the total sales to past sales experience and the planner should divide this by total estimated sales potential so as to determine the number of sales territories required. After making these estimates contiguous control units are combined into tentative sales territories of roughly equal sales potential.

### 4. Adjusting for Differences in Coverage Difficulty and Redistricting Tentative Sales Territories

The fourth and final step involved in the procedures for setting up new sales territories or revising the existing sales territories is to redistrict the tentative sales territories by making necessary adjustments for differences in coverage difficulties. Each tentative sales territory should include approximately the same potentials ignoring the relative difficulties involved in sales coverage. It is almost certain that each sales territory differs in making selling efforts required realizing the same sales potential. For example, certain big cities like Delhi, Calcutta, Mumbai, Chennai and Jaipur provide large sales potentials for most products at lower selling cost as compared to small cities which have less sales potential along with comparatively high selling costs. The optimum sales territorial arrangement should be achieved in achieving this itself Both sales potential and coverage difficulty must be considered and territoritial adjustments should be made by adding the same in the other terminative sales territory. The final territorial arrangement shall be one in which individual salesman should act. It should be done in accordance with the capability of each salesman. However, one thing is certain that none of the salesmen should be entrusted with more than the maximum desired workload.

In this way the above four steps will facilitate in establishing new sales territories or revising the existing sales territories. Revision of sales territories is a continuous process and hence the planner should be ready to re- district the existing sales territories and making necessary adjustments as and when required.

## ADVANTAGES OR IMPORTANCE TO THE ENTERPRISE

(1) Market potentiality of each sales territory can be more fully tapped.

(2) Activities of each salesman can be more effectively planned, compared, controlled and evaluated.

(3) A fair wage for evaluating salesman's performance could be geared to his compensation plan.

(4) It provides incentive to salesman to increase sales in his territory.

(5) Salesman can be held responsible individually for their activities and necessary action can also be taken accordingly.

(6) Information about change in the taste and fashion etc. from each sales territory may be gathered promptly.

(7) It facilitates comparison of the performance of different salesmen in different territories.

(8) It becomes easier to equalize the workload of each salesman

(9) Sales efforts can be more easily planned and duplication and overlapping of efforts of salesmen are avoided. In this way, the selling expenses can be reduced considerably.

(10) Due to establishment of sales territories the work of marketing research becomes easy.

(11) Sales are increased on account of the establishment of sales territories.

(12) Increased sales lead to the increase in profits of the enterprise.

(13) The effect of advertisement and sales promotion can be easily measured.

(14) It helps the sales manager to plan proper and efficient routing of salesmen so as to provide even coverage.

(15) It facilitates market research work.

(16) Inefficient salesmen are forced to either improve or quit.

## ADVANTAGES OR IMPORTANCE TO THE CUSTOMERS

1. Complaints of customers can be promptly attended to by the salesman of the concerned sales territory.
2. Personal attention can be given to the individual customer
3. Regular and more efficient service to the customers can be offered within the sales territory.
4. Production can be adjusted according to taste, fashion and suggestions of the customers.
5. More effective coverage of customers can be done through adequate number and quality of salesman's cells.

## ADVANTAGES OR IMPORTANCE TO THE SALESMAN

1. Honest, sincere and hard working salesmen have bright chances of making progress and getting easy promotions etc.
2. Equal workload is assigned to salesmen. Hence they are free from the problem of excessive workload.
3. The salesmen remain in close contact with their customer, which plays a positive role in increasing sales.
4. Separate sales territories provide an opportunity to the salesmen of showing their ability, competence and efficiency to the sales manager.
5. It encourages hard work and creative efforts on the part of salesmen.

## REVIEW QUESTIONS

1. What are Sales fields?
2. What are Sales Territories?
3. Why a Sales territory has to be established/revised?
4. State the objects of establishing sales territory?
5. Explain the reasons for revising sales territories
6. State the factors affecting sales territory
7. Explain the consideration to be kept in mind before allocating a sales territory?
8. Explain various methods of establishing sales territory
9. Explain the advantages of sales territories to (a) enterprise (b) customers and (c) salesmen.

# 5 Sales Quotas

## MEANING AND DEFINITION OF SALES QUOTA

In addition to allocating sales territories to obtain adequate control it is essential for the sales manager to fix adequate sales quota for the individual salesman to be achieved during a given period. Sales quota is the estimated or pre-determined volume or value of sales expected to be achieved by the sales force over a given period of time. It is a quantitative assignment of objective to be achieved specifically by a unit. In absolute terms, sales quota is set for an individual salesman "Sales goal assigned to a marketing unit is to be achieved specifically by a unit in absolute terms. Sales quota is set for an individual salesman and a market segment or a territory. Sales quota may be defined as "Sales goal assigned to a marketing unit to be used for managing the sales effort. " According to Paul H.Nystrom, *"A sales quota is a part of a company's total estimated sales assigned to a salesman, a territory, a branch, a distributor or dealer or to some other selling unit, as a goal to be attained in a designated future period of time"*. According to Still, Cundiff and Govoni, *"Quotas are quantitative objectives to sales personnel and other units of the selling organization."*

Sales quota can be expressed in terms of rupees or in physical units. The marketing unit for which the sales quota is set may be an individual salesman, a territory, a branch, a district, a region, a state, a dealer or even a customer. Most often, sales quotas are fixed for each marketing unit for a fixed period say for one year and then are divided on monthly basis or even weekly basis. A sales quota is very useful for the checking of the efficiency of an individual salesman or a group of salesmen. Setting up of adequate sales quotas makes it easier to specified standards. Actual performance is compared with the quota standards so set. Such comparison provides the management to control the sales force performance.

(*i*) To maximize sales in physical as well as in monetary terms.
(*ii*) To facilitate distribution of sales to various market segments and territories.
(*iii*) To ensure a systematic and rational physical distribution of products.
(*iv*) To make the best use of available sales force by fixing sales quotas in accordance with the efficiency and experience of the sales force.

## FACTORS DETERMINING SALES QUOTA

The desired profits can be achieved only if the sales quotas are adequately fixed. For example, if unattainable sales quotas are fixed the salesman may become nervous and thus may give up making necessary effort. Hence before fixing the sales quotas, it is essential to study the factors, which determine sales quotas. They are as follows :

### 1. Past Sales:

The sales quota for the next year may be fixed on the basis of sales done during the last year and after making necessary adjustments in view of changed circumstance, if any.

**2. Potentialities of the Market:**

Potentialities of the market are an important factor in determining sales quota. consumer's taste, nature, fashion, customer's purchasing power, extent of competition, climatic conditions and the policy of the government etc. Are such factors, affect the amount of sales to a great extent? After analyzing these factors marketing possibilities of the entire industry should be calculated. Afterwards the total sales target of the enterprise should be fixed. In the end, this sales target should be distributed amongst the different sales territories keeping in view their existing local prevailing conditions.

**3. Production Capacity**

While determining the salesquota, the production capacity of the enterprise should also be kept in mind. If the enterprise intends to increase its production capacity then the sales quota will have to be increased to that extent.

**4. Advertising and Sales Promotion:**

Advertising and sales promotion policy is also an important factor, which should also be kept in mind while determining the sales quota of an enterprise. If the enterprise adopts aggressive advertising and sales promotion policy in a particular sales region or sales territory then the enterprise may fix the high sales quota for that region or territory.

**5. Product Development**

The policy of the enterprise towards product development also affects the sales quota. If the enterprise is carrying on product development programme on a wide scale then the sales quota can be increased to that extent.

**6. Level of Competition**

Level of competition is also an important factor, which affects the fixation of sales quota of an enterprise. If the enterprise is facing keen competition along with the entry of few fresh, new competitors in the market then the sales are bound to be affected and hence a lower sales quota may be fixed. On the contrary, if the enterprise is having a monopolistic position then a higher sales quota may be fixed.

**7. Living Standard of the Consumers:**

Living standard of the consumers of the region concerned is also an important factor, which should be kept in mind while determining the sales quota of that region. If the standard of living of the consumers residing in a particular region is high then a higher sales quota may be fixed for that particular region.

**8. Sales Forecasting :**

Sales forecasting is also an important factor, which should be kept in mind while fixing the sales quota of the region. If the wholesalers, retailers and travelling agents are forecasting that the future prospects of marketing are very bright in a particular region then the enterprise may fix a higher sales quota for that particular region.

**9. Sales Policy**

Sales policy of the enterprise is also an important factor in determining the size of the sales quota. If the policy of the enterprise is to increase sales by adopting some new sales promotion techniques such as increase in discount rates, extension of credit policy, arranging sales contests, etc, then a higher sales quota may be fixed.

**10. Government Policy**

While determining the sales quota of an enterprise the policy of the government towards the industry should also be kept in mind. If the policy of the government is to provide encouragement to the industry by giving several concessions and exemptions etc., then a higher sales quota may be fixed.

## METHODS OF DETERMINING SALES QUOTAS

The sales quota of an enterprise may be determined in many ways. However, the basic methods of determining sales quotas are as follows:

- Executive Opinion Method
- Past Performance Method
- Sales Force Composite Method

**1. Executive Opinion Method :**

Under this method the managers or executives of the organization combine their experience and judgment to establish the sales quotas. In this way several specialized viewpoints can be brought to bear on determining the sales quota. This is also called as the "guess work" quota method as it is entirely based on the executive's thinking or guesswork.

**2. Past Performance Method :**

Under this method the sales quota is based purely on the past sales of the enterprise. The past figure is taken as the base and keeping in view the prevailing conditions in the market, it is decided to increase or decrease the sales volume by a certain percentage so as to arrive at the total sales quota for the next year. Thereafter it is divided into different sales territories, products and salesmen.

**3. Sales Force Composite Method :**

Under this method the responsibility of setting sales quota is fixed on the sales force including sole agents, dealers, distributors, branch/regional managers and the salesmen working in different sales territories. They provide their own opinion in a conference with the executive such as sales manager. Both these methods attempt to look at past performance and future possibilities of the market. All the figures so collected are totalled accordingly. The total sales quota of the enterprise is generally broken down into sales territories and individual sales quotas.

Whatever method is used in arriving at the sales quota, it is necessary to sell to the sales force the idea of the sales quota system and the quota itself for it to work efficiently. Further, salesmen should be informed by the sales manager from time to time regarding their actual performances and deviations, if any, from the sale quotas fixed, sales territories appropriately and also to provide for adequate routing so that the territories are covered effectively by the concerned salesman in the least possible time.

## THE VARIOUS TYPES OF SALES QUOTAS

According to Still, Gundiff and Govoni,

Sales volume quotas can be classified as:

1. Sales Volume Quotas derived mainly from territorial sales potential estimates.
2. Sales volume quotas derived mainly from total market estimates.
3. Sales volume quotas based on executives or sales manager's judgment alone.
4. Sales volume quotas rated to salesman compensation plan.

5. Sales volume quotas set by sales personnel themselves.
6. Budget Quotas which can be classified as:
   (a) Sales expense quotas.
   (b) Gross margin or net profit quotas
   (c) Activity Quotas
   (d) Combination and Other Point System Quotas.

## 1. SALES VOLUME QUOTAS

This is the oldest, easiest and most common type of setting sales quota system. Under this system the sales manager makes aware to the salesmen about their performances, which he wants to be achieved during a given period. Sales volume quotas are fixed on (i) Geographical area basis, (ii) Product basis, or (iii) on Marketing channel basis or on one or more of these in combination with any unit of sales organization. Generally this system of setting sales quota is more easy and effective in case of small selling units.

'The following bases are used for setting sales volume quota

### 1. Sales Volume Quotas Derived mainly from Territorial Sales Estimates

It seems logical that a sales volume quota should be derived from sales potential of a given territory. The sales potential in a territory means the maximum sales opportunities available to the same selling unit. Thus the sales potential for a product or product line in a given sales territory is taken into consideration for setting the sales volume quotas. This approach may prove fruitful in two situations:

(*i*) When total sales estimates are distributed proportionally in different sales regions or sales territories, when regional sales estimates are based on such factors as fast sales, competition, changing market conditions, differences in personnel ability, changes in prices and products and sales promotion techniques etc.

(*ii*) Sales Volume Quotas Derived from Total Market Estimates

In most of the cases sales territories are equal except with minor differences. While determining sales quotas on regional basis, information about (i) purchasing power index, and (ii) actual sales is utilized. The actual sales during a given period are compared with the sales quota assigned for that particular period and the difference, if any, is calculated. Afterwards causes of difference are analyzed and on this basis the New Year's sales quota is assigned or fixed.

### 2. Sales Volume Quotas Based on Past Sales Experience Alone

Setting sales volume quotas for the territories in question are based on the past sales performance and sales experience. One method of setting sales volume quota for each territory is to increase the last year's sales quota with an arbitrary percentage or with an arbitrary amount. Another method may be to make use of the average sales of past several years as the base and then to increase them with an arbitrary percentage or an arbitrary amount of sales and thus set sales volume quotas. The latter is better because it uses the sales trend and assumes that past and future sales are related and past sales records are satisfactory.

However, this method of using past sales as the basis for setting sales volume quotas is seldom used in modern days.

### II. Sales Volume Quotas Based on Executive's or Sales Manager's Judgment Alone

In this system, executives or sales manager's judgment is used in setting sales volume quotas. This system is justified only when there is little or no information with the executive or sales manager to use in setting sales quotas. It might be possible that the product or market or sales territory or salesman may be quite new. Under these or similar circumstances the executive or the sales manager has no choice except to take arbitrary judgment for setting sales volume quotas. The success of this system of setting sales volume quota is doubtful, as it does not provide any incentive to the salesman.

*1. Sales Volume Quotas Based on Compensation Plan*

Under this system sales volume quotas are based totally on compensation plan. Other factors like territorial sales potentials, total market potentials, past sales experience etc. are not considered at all in fixing the compensation of sales force. Sales volume quotas are tailored exclusively to fit the compensation plan. This system of setting sales volume quotas is not popular in modern age.

*2. Sales Volume Quotas Set by Sales Personnel themselves*

Many enterprises turn the problem of setting sales volume quotas over to the sales personnel themselves who are supposed to have better knowledge of their own performance as they are in close touch with each other. Each salesman is entrusted with the work of fixing his own sales quota. The argument of the executive or the sales manager behind this plan is that customers, knows them best and thereby he can set the most realistic sales volume quotas. The sales volume quota set by the individual salesman will be more realistic, fair and attainable.

### III. Budget Quotas

Budget Quotas are set for various units in the sales organization for controlling selling expenses and gross margin or net profit. The intention behind setting budget quotas is to make the sales personnel know that their job is not only to increase the volume of sales but also to increase the gross margin or net profit. Budget quotas can be classified as under:

*1. Sales Expenses Quotas*

Under this system sales expenses are determined for each sales territory by the sales manager. Such determination is done either by allotting sales expenses in lump sum or in proportion of sales volume or in proportion of gross margin or net profit. The idea behind this system is to make the individual salesman more cost-conscious and aware of his responsibility to control selling expenses.

*2. Gross Margin or Net Profit Quotas*

Gross Margin or net profit quotas are set when product, consists of high and low margin items. Low margin items can be easily sold and hence salesmen may concentrate on low margin items only. On the contrary, since it is difficult to sell more profitable items salesmen might give inadequate attention to the sale of more profitable items. Hence in order to face this vital problem gross margin and net profit quota system is adopted. In this case sales volume quotas for different products for each salesman are set, adjusting each quota to obtain the desired margin of profits.

*3. Activity Quotas*

Some sales manager set sales quotas for the activities of their sales personnel in order to control and allocation of time to the sales personnel. A sales manager using such quota system defines the various activities, which are commonly performed by the sales personnel, and also sets target performance frequencies. The activities for which sales quotas are fixed are total sales calls, product demonstrations, placement of displays, number of new accounts, missionary calls, efforts to make collections and the like. The sales manager takes the assistance of 'time and duty studies' before setting activity quotas. However, if activities quotas are appropriate then the sales personnel also perform non-selling activities.

Setting activities quotas involves large amount of clerical and record keeping work. The main danger of this system is that the sales personnel may simply go through the movement only, i.e., showing that they are doing excessive activities or work whereas they are not actually performing even primary activities effectively. According to G.Ristey, "Activity quotas alone can reward salesman for quantity of work, irrespective of quality for a dangerously long time. "

### IV. Combination and other Point System Quotas

When determination of sales, quota is based on several points, it is called, 'combination and other point system quotas." Combination quota system is prepared after giving due weight-age to the volume of sales, having obtained new customers, contact or call to prospects and product demonstration etc. By this method it is possible to have combined percentage evaluation of all the efforts of the salesman. Performances against combination quotas are computed as percentages. Such quotas are also known as point systems, the point being percentage points.

## THE REQUISITES OF SUCCESSFUL QUOTA SYSTEM

### 1. Accurate, Fair and Attainable Quotas:

The first and the foremost requisite of a successful quota system is that the quota assigned to a salesman must be accurate, fair and attainable. Setting unrealistic and non-attainable quota creates problems both to the salesman and the sales administration. Whether a particular quota is accurate, fair and attainable depends equally on the capabilities and motivation of sales force.

### 2. Securing and Maintaining the Sales Force Acceptance

Mere setting of quotas is meaningless unless they are clearly understood and acceptable to the salesman concerned who is expected to work on them.

### 3. Participating in Quota Setting

Quotas should not be set behind the curtain. In fixing and setting sales quotas, the sales-force should be taken into confidence. The sales quotas are rendered easier if the sales department allows salesmen's participation while setting quotas.

### 4. Keeping the Sales – force Informed of their Attainment

Simply setting quotas is not enough. The management should keep the sales – force informed of its progress actually achieved in realizing the targets set from time to time. Each salesman should get his report as to what extent this progress is comparable to the quotas set-how much? In what time? Such a comparison permits the investigation of the causes of success or failure so that corrective action can be taken well in time.

### 5. Continuous Managerial Control

Finally, there must be continuous managerial control about the actual performance of the sales-force and the achievement of sales quotas to be set. Timely information regarding the actual performance and achievement may be weekly, fortnightly or monthly depending on the requirements of the system of control. As quotas setting conditions differ and abilities differ, necessary changes can be implemented by keeping the system flexible.

## THE ADVANTAGES AND DISADVANTAGES OF SETTING SALES QUOTAS

Sales quotas are an important tool in the hands of the executive or sales manager so as to have an effective control over the sales personnel and the selling costs. It is a control device on the basis of which sales personnel performance may be measured. The main advantages of determining sales quotas are as follows:

1. **Evaluation of Sales Performance**: It is a useful device for evaluating the performance effectiveness and productivity of the salesman. The sales quota system provides a yardstick against which such performance and effectiveness can be measured. The actual performance of the salesman is compared with the sales quota or expected performance.
2. **Locate Weak and Underdeveloped Areas**: It becomes easier to locate weak and underdeveloped market areas in terms of sales quotas for such territories.
3. **Control Device**: It is a control device, which may be used for controlling the activities of a salesman.
4. **Conduct of Sales Contests**: Sales quotas are also useful in connection with the conduct of sales contests. Prizes to salesman etc. may be awarded on the basis of how far the particular sales quota was achieved rather than in terms of mere sales volume.
5. **Effective Compensation Plan**: A more effective compensation plan may be devised on the basis of sales quota system.
6. **Controlling Selling Costs**: It may be used for controlling selling costs.
7. **Source of Motivation**: Sales quotas are the source of motivation to right type of salesmen.
8. **Maximization of Sales and Profits** : Sales quotas – their attainment will mean increase in sales and there by increase in profits also. Profit maximization is possible only when there is maximization of sales.

## DISADVANTAGES OR DEMERITS OR LIMITATIONS OF SALES QUOTA SYSTEM

1. **Based on Arbitrary Estimates :** Most of the sales quotas are based on arbitrary estimates and past experience and thus they prove misleading on several occasions.
2. **Danger of ineffectiveness:** If the salesmen feel that the sales quotas for them have been fixed in his ivory tower by persons at the head offices who are absolutely unaware of the salesmen's problems, the motivating aspect of sales quotas would be lost.
3. **Problem of Quota Fixing:** Setting sales quota requires a statistical technique, which is not easy to explain to the sales force or to be understood by them.
4. **Apply of Discord :** Unattainable or high sales quotas encourage high pressure selling which is harmful. It causes frustration to salesman who is likely to give up making the necessary effort.
5. **Short Supply** : In those enterprises in which the product is in short supply, it is useless to determine the sales quota because the product is automatically sold. There is absolutely no problem of selling the product.

6. **Too Low Quota :** The interest and the incentive of the salesman is lost if the sales quota is too low.
7. **Other Field Remain Untouched :** Some executives oppose sales quotas on the ground that too much emphasis is laid on making sales, other fields remain untouched, which is harmful from the point of view of the future growth of the enterprise.
8. **Wastage of Time, Energy and Money :** Some executives feel that determination of sales quota is a wastage of time, energy and money. It is an expensive device.
9. **Danger of Increased Bad Debts :** In the high hope of selling more and more so as to achieve quota targets, it is feared that the salesman may resort to the tactics of granting very liberal terms, such as sale on credit, and thereby putting the business enterprise in the trap of increased bad debts.

## THE RELATIONSHIP BETWEEN SALES QUOTAS, SALES FORECAST AND SALES BUDGET

As a matter of fact, the sales quota, the sales forecast and the sales budget are closely connected with each other. However; their relationship differs from company to company, depending upon the degree of integration. The greater the degree of integration the more potential effectiveness quotas have as a device for controlling sales efforts.

Sales efforts begin with the sales forecasting leading to formulation of the sales budget. Basically, a sales forecast is an estimate of sales during a given period of time after estimating the probable selling expenses of obtaining this sales level. Afterwards, the sales management computes the indicated net profit contribution. All these figures are incorporated in a sales budget. Afterwards the total sales quota of the company is fixed. In the end the same is assigned to individual sales personnel or to other organizational units of sales department or to distributive outlets

## REVIEW QUESTIONS

1. What are Sales Quotas?
2. How a Sales Quota can be expressed?
3. Bring out the methods is determining sales quota
4. What do you mean by Sales volume quota?
5. Explain the factors determining Sales Quota
6. What are various types of Sales Quotas?
7. Briefly explain the requisites for a successful quota system.
8. State the merits and demerits offsetting Sales Quotas.
9. How sales quotas, sales forecast and sales budget are related with each other!
10. What are sales budget quotas!

# 6 Salesman's Report

If a sales manager intends to manage, direct and control the activities of the salesmen who are scattered all over the different territories throughout the country, he must get requisite information as to their movements, the customers or prospects they have visited and the conditions of the sales in their respective territories regularly. He should also know whether the proper movement of goods is taking place, who are the old and new customers and whether they are satisfied with the products of the firm and the service. He must have also information with regard to the complaints of the customers so that he can readily attend to them. He might have also launched upon a programme of sales promotion. He would be interested in knowing how far it has succeeded. Since the salesman is the person who is actually on the spot, he makes a report about all these activities to the sales manager. Thus the report of the salesman is the mirror of the sales position in the whole of the sales area. Salesman's report is a source of communication between the salesman and the sales manager. It provides the requisite information required by the sales manager about the activities of the salesmen. It also assists the sales manager in determining what more can be done to secure more and larger orders and also to win the confidence of the salesman and the customers. Salesman's report provides the raw materials that sales manager makes use of, for gaining insights, which provide background materials for evaluation purposes.

## OBJECTIVES OR PURPOSES OF SALESMAN'S REPORT

The general purpose of salesman's report is to provide requisite information needed for evaluating the performance of the sales personnel. Besides this; the report also contains additional information, which is generally used by the sales manager for other administrative purposes. The main objectives or purposes of salesman's report are as follows.

1. To evaluate the performance of individual salesmen
2. To control the activities of the salesmen.
3. To gather or collect information of competitor's activities.
4. To record customer's reactions – Reports contain Information about customer's complaints, suggestions, reactions about new products, price changes, price polices, service policies, advertising campaigns etc.
5. To find out the problems of salesmen and give necessary assistance in solving those problems.
6. To report changes in local and business conditions
7. To have comparative study of salesmen's activities.
8. To acquire necessary information, data etc. for marketing research.

9. To collect necessary information, data etc. for marketing research.
10. To assist the sales personnel in planning their activities.

## UTILITY OF SALESMAN'S REPORT

**The salesman's report is, of great utility both to the company and the salesman himself. They may be summarized as an order.**

1. The sales manager may form, change or amend his policies, practices and programmes on the basis of salesmen's reports.
2. The progress and the performance of the salesmen may be evaluated both qualitatively and quantitatively on the basis of these reports.
3. It is a way of increasing sales and making it easier for the salesmen to sell.
4. By insisting on submission of report by the salesman, the usual habit of self-analysis and analyzing his territory is also developed in the salesman
5. Information about competitors activities can be acquired through salesmen's reports. The sales manager may make necessary changes in policies and products etc. to meet the challenges of the market
6. Decision about providing credit facilities to the customers can be taken on the basis of salesmen's reports
7. Necessary coordination between sales and production can be established on the basis of salesmen's reports
8. Effective control on salesmen can be established on the basis of their reports
9. Sales promotion policies can be evaluated on the basis of salesmen's reports
10. Alteration in sales territories can be done on the basis of salesmen's reports
11. Necessary changes in the current product line with regard to packing; colour, size, design, price etc. can be made on the basis of salesmen's reports
12. From the salesman's report, it is possible to estimate the selling costs.
13. Salesman's report helps in the preparation of customer's records.
14. Salesmen's reports are very helpful to the office in planning salesman's journey.
15. Salesmen's reports are of immense value in conducting market research.
16. Salesmen's reports assist the sales manager to evaluate the difficulties encountered by the different salesmen in their work, and if possible, to assist them in the way he can.

## TYPES OF SALESMAN'S REPORTS:

The various types of salesmen's report through which the activities may be controlled are of various types. It depends on the shape and size of business and business enterprise. However, salesman's report may be of the following types.

### 1. Progress or Call Report

Every salesman prepares this report individually either for each call or cumulatively covering all calls made during a fixed period, say every day or week. Progress or call reports keep sales management aware of the salesmen's activities, provide first hand information about the standing of the company with individual account, and in different territories and also record the information which might assist the sales person on his revisits to customers and prospects. It contains almost all necessary information not only about sales or orders but also specific class of present and future customers, competitive brands handled, strength and activities of competitors, best time to call on customers and above all promises made by the prospects for future purchases. Almost all business enterprises make use of progress or call report.

**2. Sales – work Plan Report**

The salesman about his future work plan submits this report for a specified future period, say a week or a month. This report contains such details as accounts and prospects to be called upon, products and other matters to be discussed, future traveling programmes along with routes to be travelled, proposed hotels and motels, publicity and contacts to be done etc. The main purpose of this report is to help the salesman in planning and scheduling his activities and also to keep the sales management informed of his whereabouts. The specimen of Sales-work Plan Report is given below.

**MAHINDRA AND MAHINDRA, PUNE**

Name of Salesman ———————— Date ———————— Week————————

| Day | Name of the Prospect | Place | Object of Visit |
|---|---|---|---|
| Monday | | | |
| Tuesday | | | |
| Wednesday | | | |
| Thursday | | | |
| Friday | | | |
| Saturday | | | |

**3. Expense Report**

Monthly sales personnel are reimbursed for all the expenses incurred by them in performing their job. Hence they are required to submit detailed item-wise expense report stating their nature and the amounts of expenses for the purpose of general administrative control and also for income tax assessments. Such reports help the sales management to control the nature and account of sales personnel expenses. This report also helps the sales personnel to exercise self-control on expenses. Sales personnel periodical expense reports remind them to be under moral obligation to keep their expense in line with their – reported sales volumes. This report is to be submitted mostly weekly. This report also assists the sales management to control over sales personnel and also to control sales expenses in line with sales volumes. The specimen of expense report is given below:

**INDOGEN GOPAL COMPANY, CHENNAI**

Name of the Salesman ..............................Date..................Week..............

| *Date/ Day* | *Name of the Place* | *Food Expenses* | *Residential Expenses* | *Entertain ment* | *Misc. Exp,* | *Daily Total* | *Remarks* |
|---|---|---|---|---|---|---|---|
| Monday | | | | | | | |
| Tuesday | | | | | | | |
| Wednesday | | | | | | | |
| Thursday | | | | | | | |
| Friday | | | | | | | |
| Saturday | | | | | | | |
| | Total | | | | | | |

Re Imbursed Amount

I verify that the above expenses were legally incurred in connection with business object only.

Signature.................

Approval.....................

**4. New Businesses or Potential New Business Report:**

This report contains detail as to new customers and prospects who may become company's new source of 'business'. It provides data to the sales management for evaluating the extent and effectiveness of development work, particularly new business carried on by sales personnel. The other purpose of this report is to remind the sales personnel not to confine themselves to old and well-established customers only but also regularly contact prospects to make them regular customers of the company's products. On the basis of this report, the sales management may evaluate the effectiveness of prospecting. That is way it is also called 'Activity Report'.

**5. Lost Sales Report**

This report contains information about the customers and the orders lost during a given period. This report gives a detailed account of the reasons for the loss of business and also the comments of the sales personnel. On the basis of this report, the sales management tries to prevent the future possible loss in sales. It guides the sales management to point out the way to needed sales training changes in customer service, product improvement and also to check and investigate the irresponsibility's of the sales personnel.

**6. Report of Complaint and / or Adjustment**

It is also an important report which contains various complaints received and/or adjusted about company's products, selling policies, service deficiencies, pricing, sales techniques and practices etc. The report provides information needed for analyzing the nature and volume of complaints arising from an individual salesman's work, the incidence of specific complaints by class of customers and cost of complaint adjusted. This report also assists the sales management in detecting needed product improvements, changes in merchandising and service practices and sales policies etc. The specimen of this is given below:

## MAHAVIR JAIN, SRIPERUMPUDUR

Date ......................

Name of the Customer........... Address................ Phone No.......

Specific Description

Product Problems : ☐

Order not supplied : ☐

Defective goods : ☐

Defective quality : ☐

Repairs Problem : ☐

Wrong goods supplied : ☐

Credit not adjusted : ☐

Others : ☐

Delivery Problems : ☐

Wrong Address : ☐

Customer not available : ☐

Loss in transit : ☐

Damaged in transit : ☐

Goods not received : ☐

Packing Problem : ☐

Others : ☐

Solution to the Problem : ☐

## REVIEW QUESTIONS

1. What is a Sales Report?
2. State the General Purpose of a Salesman's Report
3. State the main purpose of Sales work plan report
4. State the objectives or purposes of a salesman's report
5. Explain various types of Salesman reports.

# 7 Selling Process

## MEANING OF SELLING PROCESS

In primitive days demand preceded the supply and therefore, there was no need to make any effort to sell one's own products. But as there is progress in society, production is no longer carried on, on a small scale but on a large scale. Even one product is produced not by one producer but by several producers, such as cotton textiles, steel, shoes, paper etc. It results in overproduction and competition among the producers. When this happens, it is no longer necessary for the consumer to go to the producer and place his demand. What actually happens is that the producer goes to the consumer to book his demand.

In this way, the consumer becomes the 'king'. The producer follows different steps, one by one so as to persuade the consumer to buy his product that will give him satisfaction. Theses steps are known as stages of selling process. In other words, the steps taken by the salesman to perform his function of selling successfully are included in selling process and thus the whole process is known as selling process.

## STAGES OR STEPS IN SELLING PROCESS

The selling process is composed of the following seven stages or steps

1. Prospecting
2. Pre-approach
3. Approach
4. Presentation and Demonstration
5. Handling or Meeting Objections
6. Closing the Sale
7. Follow-up

### 1. Prospecting

Prospecting is the first and the foremost step in the selling process. Prospecting means identifying and locating potential buyers. It helps in planning the whole selling efforts so that there is no or minimum of wasted calls. Regular and systematic prospecting is the foundation of all selling.

### 2. Pre-approach

Pre-approach is the second step in the selling process. The salesman is to acquire enough information about such prospects in order to approach each one in the most effective manner. This constitutes the 'pre-approach'. Pre-approach involves developing an understanding about those prospective buyers who have been identified and on whom the salesman proposes to call. This understanding may relate to buyers' needs, personality drafts and behavior patterns which are critical to their buying decision. Pre - approach prepares effective background of making approach ascertains the best and the most effective method of approaching the prospect. For instance, a doctor before prescribing any medicine diagnises the disease of the patient. The architect studies the plan of the land along with the needs of the client before designing a functionally efficient structure. Similar is the case with the salesman, who before starting his approach, plans the approach and, therefore, this process is known as pre-approach.

### 3. Approach

Approach is the third step or stage in the selling process; When the salesman comes in actual contact with the prospect or likely customer, the next stage, namely, the 'approach' is reached. The face-to-face contact with the prospect is termed as approach. It involves use of different methods for seeking an access to the prospect so that the product/offer may be presented to him.

### 4. Presentation and Demonstration :

It is the fourth step or stage in the selling process. In this step, the salesman demonstrates to the customer the need-satisfying characteristics of the products being offered for sale. The objective of presentation and demonstration is to help in convincing the customer that the salesman's product is the best one for satisfying his needs. In this way, effective presentation and demonstration plays a vital role in the selling process. Amongst the ways suggested for effective demonstration, the most accepted one is the AIDA approach. According to this approach, the product should be demonstrated in such a manner that it gains the customer's attention, holds his interest builds up his desire for the product, and ends up in purchase action.

### 5. Meeting or Handling Objections

It is the fifth step in the selling process. Raising objections is a normal feature of the selling process. Under this step the salesman is required to handle and over come objections arising during or as a result of presentation and demonstration. It is just natural for the customer to ask questions, raise objections and seek explanation. It is the most difficult situation that a salesman is required to face. The salesman's job is to effectively meet, handle and answer them in a most convincing and systematic manner.

### 6. Closing the Sales

It is the sixth step in the selling process. It means request for getting an order. After having answered and overcome objections, it is the right time for the salesman to clinch the deal by closing the demonstration. The object of closing the sale is to get the customer in the mood of saying 'yes' so that the salesman can ask for the order. Thus closing the sale is also a very important step of the selling process. The salesman is expected to perform the same in a very decent manner.

### 7. Follow – Up

It is the last step and equally important step in selling process. After closing, it is important for the salesman to follow up the order booked so as to ensure that the order is properly executed. Follow-up is also necessary to gather information from the customers regarding product use problems, if any, and the level of customer satisfaction. It builds up goodwill, ensures feedback and encourages repeated purchases.

## PROSPECTING

Just as the prospector in case of mining explores with a view to finding valuable mineral deposits, in the same way the salesman looks for and explores valuable prospects, that is, persons who are in need of his product. The need can be converted into want and the same may finally be converted into purchases. Prospecting means finding out qualified and potential customers. In other words, prospecting is the method of finding out the prospects or likely customers. Actually selling process starts with prospecting. Regular and systematic prospecting is the foundation of all selling. A salesman is constantly on the lookout for prospects, which means he is looking out for individuals, whom he can ultimately convert into buyers. In this case, we must remember that prospecting is not a wild goose chase. It is a systematic and continuous search of a potential customer.

## CHARACTERISTICS OF A GOOD PROSPECT

Prospecting is as wide as a desert; but it does not mean that because it is desert, oil can be found everywhere. Prospects are too many, for that reason every human being may be considered as a prospect. But this concept is wrong. It is not correct to consider everyone to be a prospect without first determining whether these individuals possess the necessary characteristics of a good prospect. Thus it is most essential for an efficient salesman to know the characteristics of a good prospect. In this connection the main characteristics of a good prospect are as follows:

### 1. Does the Prospect Have a Need?

The first and the foremost characteristic of a good prospect is that he must have the need of the product. A need must exist which is capable of being converted into a want and a want into purchase. In case the prospect does not have the need of the product in question then it is the responsibility of the salesman to see that the need is created by means of creative salesmanship.

### 2. Does the Prospect have Ability to Pay?

The second characteristic of a good prospect is that he should have the ability to pay. Because if wishes were horses even beggars could ride them. Mere desire or want is not sufficient. It must be an effective want duly backed by the ability to pay. Ability to pay means possessing enough financial resources to make the payment.

### 3. Does the Prospect have Ability to Sacrifice?

Simply having a want and ability to pay is not enough; the prospect should also have the ability to sacrifice. For instance, take the case of a miser. He possesses both, i.e. the want and the ability to pay but the ability to sacrifice is lacking. Thus his desire or want cannot be converted into purchase.

### 4. Does the Prospect have the Authority to Buy?

The fourth characteristic of a good prospect is that he should have the requisite authority to buy. For instance, the son of a rich businessman desires a car but he does not have the requisite authority from his father to buy a car. In this case the salesman should approach the father and not the son for selling the car.

### 5. Is the Prospect Approachable?

Really speaking, a big gap exists between a high, executive authority and the salesman, that of approachability. The salesman is required to cross many hurdles before approaching the high executive. The salesman should take into consideration, the nature, the status and the circle etc. of the high executive before making any approach to him.

### 6. Is the Prospect Eligible to Buy?

The last but not the least important characteristic of a good prospect is that he should be eligible to buy. For instance, certain goods can be sold only to a licence-holder, such as gun or pistol, or at the recommendation of a qualified doctor, such as medicine.

From the above discussions, it is evident that a good prospect is one who has the need to buy, has ability to pay, is prepared to sacrifice, has authority to buy, and is approachable and also eligible to buy.

## METHODS OF PROSPECTING OR SEARCHING FOR THE PROSPECTS

The salesmen from time to time for prospecting or searching the prospects are employing different methods. The important methods which are usually employed for prospecting by the salesmen are as follows:

### 1. Cold-Canvass Method

The cold-canvass method or, as is popularly known in America, 'Cold-turkey calling', is also resorted to by salesmen to increase the number of their prospects. In this method a salesman prepares a list of individuals or firms who are most likely to purchase his product on certain presumptions. For instance, let us suppose that an office stationery salesman assumes that wherever there is an office there is the need for office stationery. Having prepared the complete list of all the offices that exist in his sales territory, he starts converting each one of them on a certain plan. His plan is to visit five such offices everyday and leave his name and address behind. Within the course of a month he will have covered about 140-150 such offices. Later on, he will start making calls in those offices. It is likely that some calls may be successful and some may not. In case of unsuccessful calls, he may continue to make calls in the next month or on the appointed date and time and so on. This method is most common now-a-days. Mostly those salesmen who are hard working and untiring in energy adopt this method.

### 2. Endless Chain or Family Tree Method

Another method of increasing the number of prospects is called 'Endless Chain or Family Tree Method". This is a term applied to the process of securing an endless number of prospects. This is a very useful and popular method for securing new customers. Under this method, when a salesman interviews any customer, he secures the names of some prospects for future interviews. For instance, he may ask the customer to give names of two or three acquaintances, relatives or friends who may be interested in what he is selling. Thus one prospect leads to another and an endless chain of prospects is formed. The advantage of this method is that it is a continuous process and an intelligent salesman would in this way collect a mass of information about relatives, friends and associates etc. who may be potential customers in the near future.

### 3. Centre-of-influence Method

In this method, the salesman consults influential persons in his locality or territory such as bankers, teachers, doctors, leading politicians, business executives, club officials etc. about their acquaintances, relatives, friends etc. who may turn out to be potential customers. This method is a modification of the endless chain method.

### 4. Personal Observation Method

This is also an important method of prospecting. Just as dogs are employed by the police to find out a culprit who is guilty of some crime, similarly experienced salesmen are employed to discover a good prospect. The personal observation of the salesman for a prospect is not merely confined when he is on duty. He will remain constantly on the lookout for bits of information of value to him, whether on way to the work, in the office, at a dinner party or any social function.

### 5. Junior Salesmen and Bird Dog Method

It is also an important and popular method used by the salesman for identifying the prospects. In this method, junior salesmen are employed to call at the door of every house in a particular locality of community, inquire about the type of product which is being used, and from the reactions obtained, an attempt is made to get an appointment at a later time for the experienced salesman to explain the features of their latest product. This method is usually applied for selling costly domestic products, such as washing machines, grinding machines, refrigerator or even automobiles etc.

Bird dog' is a name given to water and electric meter readers. In this method, the salesman contacts them whom, on certain payment, give a clue as to kind of prospects residing in a particular locality. On the basis of the clue the salesman picks out certain persons only and tries to sell his product to them.

### 6. Trade Fairs, Exhibitions and Demonstrations

Participation in trade fairs and exhibitions etc. is another method of prospecting. Many companies display or demonstrate their products in trade-fairs and exhibitions 'organized at state level, country level or even world level. Care is taken to obtain names and addresses of individuals and firms etc. who appear to be interested in the company's products.

### 7. Miscellaneous Method

There are other miscellaneous methods of prospecting. They include inquiring on the telephone, use of direct mail (sending of a circular letter enclosing a return card), launching advertising campaign, using trade directories etc.

## PRE-APPROACH

Pre-approach commences as soon as the salesman obtains the name and address of the prospect. Prospecting is generally completed when the salesman feels that he knows enough about the prospect and there is a chance of selling to him. Pre-approach is a fact-finding stage of selling process in which additional information, other than that about the prospect, such as his likes and dislikes, habits, type of buying motive, economic status etc. which will enable him to plan his selling campaign intelligently. The salesman by means of pre-approach ascertains the best and the most effective method of approaching the prospect. For instance, a doctor before prescribing any medicine diagnises the disease of the client. Similar is the case with the salesman, who before starting his approach, plans the approach and, therefore, this process is known as pre-approach.

## OBJECTIVES OF PRE-APPROACH

The main objective of pre-approach is to help the salesman get further insight into the customer's needs and attitude so that he can select the best approach for the individual prospect. Through the pre-approach the salesman would know the prospect's likes and dislikes as well as his preferences. The pre-approach would provide to the salesman the complete picture of the prospect well in advance. Knowing this, the salesman can treat him as he likes to be treated. The objective of the pre-approach is to provide the salesman with all the information necessary to plan his sales strategy properly. Backed with the requisite information, the salesman can meet the prospect with full confidence.

## APPROACH

Approach means meeting the prospect face to face. It is the first appearance of the salesman with the prospect. Merely pre-approach is not enough to convert a prospect into a buyer; he must see him face to face. The sales strategy is complete only when a salesman comes face to face with the prospect. The pre-approach knows things only in part and to know him fully an approach is necessary. Approach is the most critical part of the selling process. At this time the salesman should create a favourable sales impressing on the prospect. To make a favourable sales impression the salesman must look as active sales professional.

## METHODS OF MAKING APPROACH

Nowadays-different salesmen for making approach with the prospect use different methods. The important methods are as follows

### 1. The Personal Call without Introduction

In this method, a request is made by the salesman to the prospect to give him an interview at once or at a future time as may be suitable to him. He may also attempt to utilize a little psychology with some powerful motive to overcome the prospect's instinctive antagonism to a stranger. Therefore, the appeal to profit or self-interest or appeal to curiosity is commonly employed to gain the interview with the prospect.

### 2. Sending to the Business Card

In this method, the salesman to obtain an interview with the prospect uses the business card. Business cards, which have now become more or less a necessity, should have a distinctive appearance. The business card bears the name of the salesman along with the name and address of his company. In this connection one must remember that business card is not a passport to admission as it may be sent out as easily as it is sent in. It all depends on the desire of the prospect to allow admission or refuse admission.

### 3. Using the Telephone

Telephone is an effective method for securing an interview with the prospect. This method is most suitable when there are a large number of prospects. The telephone approach must be aggressive and the conversation should be speeded up after the prospect has announced his name. Opening should be made with short sentences and the sales talk on the telephone should consist of only leading questions inviting the reply 'yes'. Arguments should be totally avoided.

### 4. Writing for an Appointment

In this method, the salesman prefers to write letters to the prospects requesting appointment when he can approach them and put forward their proposition. A simple request for an appointment is likely to produce the desired result. However, the proposition must be presented in an attractive manner so that it may arouse the curiosity of the prospect.

### 5. Premiums or Door-Openers

In this method, the salesman uses premiums or door openers to obtain the interview with the prospect. Small gifts are sent to the prospect to arouse his curiosity, and make him feel under an obligation to open the door for the salesman. Such gifts usually consist of paperweights, automatic pencils, ashtrays, toothbrush, diary, calendar and similar novelties.

### 6. Introduction

Suitable introduction is one of the most effective methous of securing an interview with the prospect. In this method, the salesman approaches the prospect as an acquaintance or friend and not as a stranger. Instead of introducing himself, the salesman is required to deliver the letter or note of introduction to the prospect. Such an introduction may be obtained from a common friend, relative on acquaintance.

### 7. Sending Advance Sales Letters

In this method, sales letters are mailed in advance by the salesman's company to the prospects intimating the date and the time of arrival of their salesman to the prospect's residence or office. These letters are carefully drafted, typed and signed by the important officials of the company. It is also an important method of approaching the prospect.

### 8. The Use of 'Trickery' for Securing Appointments

This method of approach to the prospect is generally used only when the salesman, after encountering several refusals for an interview, feels certain in the mind about his ability to convert the prospect into a buyer. He may use recourse to trickery as a means of gaining the interview. The use of trickery is condemned and hence it should be used as a last resort only.

## PRESENTATION

### Meaning of Presentation

Presentation or sales presentation is a process during which the salesman tries to attract the attention and the interest of the customer towards the product. Presentation helps in convincing the customer that the salesman's product is the best one for satisfying his need. A planned presentation saves the time of the customer and the salesman. It relieves the salesman of the nervous strain and gives him the much-needed confidence. Effective sales presentation is a vital force in selling. The customer normally approaches the shop of the salesman with a vague idea of what he actually needs or wants. It is the sales presentation, which helps the customer in taking final decision for purchasing the product.

## ESSENTIALS OF SALES PRESENTATION OR EFFECTIVE SALES PRESENTATION

The following are the essentials of effective sales presentation

### 1. Promptness:

The salesman should be quite prompt in presenting the product before the customer. In order to be prompt in presentation, the salesman must have the accurate knowledge of the location of the product as desired by the customer. In case of any delay on the part of the salesman, it is likely that the customer's interest may be lost or reduced.

### 2. Clarity

The second major characteristic of effective presentation is that the sales presentation must be absolutely clear and complete. It should be so clear that no doubt is left in the customer's mind.

### 3. Showing the Proper Quality and Quantity

The third major characteristic of effective sales presentation is that the salesman should show the proper quality and quantity of the product as demanded by the customer. If the customer asks for a particular product, the salesman must immediately show the one he wants, even though another article would be more suitable for the customer.

### 4. Dramatization

The fourth major characteristic of sales presentation is dramatization. It is the art of presenting the product before the customer. The salesman must select the most effective method of dramatizing his particular product. The dramatizing is secured through visualization.

### 5. Appealing to the Senses

There are in all five senses. They are the sense of sight, sense of touch, sense of hearing, sense of smell and sense of taste. The salesman should try to appeal to all the senses of the customer.

### 6. Suggesting Tests

In order to convince the customer as to quality, the salesman should suggest the tests to the customer. For instance, wool burns with a slow flickering flame which makes it sizzle and Carl. The flame ceases as soon as it is withdrawn from the flame.

### 7. Handling the Product

Action speaks louder than words. Therefore, the salesman should demonstrate the product as much as possible. He should handle the product himself and then if possible then also permit the customer to handle the product. It is generally the habit of the customers to feel and handle the product they purchase. The customer, may therefore, be encouraged to do so.

### 8. Guarantee

The last but not the least important characteristic of effective sales presentation is to give guarantee to the customer for a certain period. For instance, salesman says to the customer, "this washing machine will give you trouble-free service for a period of two years.! During that period if the washing machine stops working he will give free service or replace it with a new washing machine. The guarantee given by the salesman relieves the customer of any doubt about the working or benefits of the product. It is essential particularly in the sale of domestic and other machinery item.

## DEMONSTRATION

According to B.R. Canfield, "Demonstration is showing with proof and example how a product or service benefits the buyer. "The objective of demonstration is to provide the customer with definite proof of the benefits as claimed by the salesman in his product. It gives the customer an opportunity to experience for himself the benefits or profits to be derived from the ownership of a product. The customer should be allowed to see, touch, feel and even operate the product for his satisfaction.

### Forms of Demonstration

The following are the two main forms of demonstration

1. **Demonstration in Use :** The most popular and effective form of demonstration is to show the customer as to how the product will appear when he actually uses it. For instance, while selling a readymade suit, the salesman should ask the customer to wear it on and look in a full-size mirror. Thus the salesman makes the customer actually see how the suit will appear on him. If the customer is pleased with the appearance, he is likely to purchase the same.

2. **Demonstration of a Specific** Feature: In case of a product, which does not lend itself to former type of demonstration, the salesman may emphasize a particular feature of that product. For instance, if a salesman is demonstrating a blotting paper, a drop of ink may be required on it from a pen to demonstrate its absorbing quality.

## TECHNIQUES OF GOOD DEMONSTRATION

The customer will be convinced only if he is sure that he will be benefited by the purchase of the product. Hence the salesman must demonstrate the product in such a way that the customer is fully convinced that the product will satisfy his need. Hence different salesmen use different techniques of sales demonstration. The main techniques of good sales demonstration are as follows.

**1. Exhibits:** Exhibit is the most popular technique of good demonstration. With the help of various visual aids like charts, diagrams, pictures etc, the salesman may convince the customer of what he has said to him about the product. Many salesmen now use audio-visual aids.

**2. Methods and Samples:** It is also an important and popular technique of good sales demonstration. In this case, the salesman shows the actual sample of the product in question to the customer. Models are used when the product to be sold is huge and large and thus cannot be presented or shown on the spot.

**3. Films and Slides:** This technique is used when the product is to be sold to a group or is costly in case of an individual. If a tourist agency desires to evoke the interest of the customers in the place or places to which the tour is to be conducted, a film show is the right answer. It must be remembered that the film should be factual and also interesting.

**4. Testimonials:** Testimonials are usually in the form of letters written by satisfied customers. These letters testify that they are fully satisfied with the product.

**5. Examples:** Citing examples of persons who are getting benefits of the products may be helpful in creating a good impression on the customer. Examples provide additional evidence of benefits and add to the reputation of the product.

**6. Miscellaneous** : (i) Demonstration should be done according to the needs of the customer. (ii) If the customer is doubtful about the benefits of a product, the salesman may offer a specific guarantee to relieve him. (iii) Product demonstration. (iv) Ability to express and to expound etc.

## THE VARIOUS METHODS OF HANDLING OBJECTIONS

A Salesman's job is not the bed of roses. To make people buy is a difficult task even when a need is established and there are adequate means to satisfy it. Most of the customers are indifferent to buying and they raise several kinds of objections when approached by the salesman. Sales resistance or objection expresses disapproval of an action. Sales resistance or objection is an outward expression, usually verbal, intended either to put off the idea of making purchases or postpone the decision to purchase of some item. It is the obstacle which prevents the customer from making a commitment. It postpones, hinders or prevents the completion of sales. An obstacle may be real or unreal or sincere or insincere. The sales resistance or rising of objections is a natural feature and normal way, which is expected, in almost all sales deals.

## METHODS OF MEETING OR HANDLING OBJECTIONS

Whatever the customer's objection may be, at least one thing is certain that the customer is taking interest in the product. Hence the first thing to do is that the salesman should listen to the customer's objections attentively and without any interruption. After he has understood them, he should think as to which method should be applied in meeting or handling the objections. In this connection there are a number of methods used by the salesman to meet and handle the objections. The most important methods are as follows.

**1. The Direct Denial Method**: Under this method, the salesman says directly on the very face of the customer that his objection is totally false or wrong. For instance, the customer makes a false-statement. Here is the syllabus and stand ready to prove this right now. Generally salesman does not use this method because it is bound to offend the customer. He might become angry and it is likely that in future he might not see your shop. This method is successful only when used by experienced and skilled salesman and that too as a sort of "desperate remedy for a desperate disease". It may be used only when the salesman feels that the statement of the customer is totally false.

**2. Indirect Denial Method**: This is most popular and widely used method of meeting objections of the customers. Under this method, the salesman agrees with the objection or objections of the customer, but then makes a statement which offsets the objection. That is why this method is also called yes, but method. For instance, our product is of much superior quality and, therefore, it will last long and thus you will save considerable money in the long run. " This method, therefore, really amounts to denying the objection tactfully without offending the customer.

**3. Boomerang Method:** The boomerang method is one where the objection raised by the customer is thrown back (returned) by the salesman in the form of a reason, why he should purchase the product. Thus the objection is converted into a reason in favour of the purchase. This method is also called as the "Translation Method because it translates the objection into a reason infavour of the purchase. For instance, when a customer raises an objection the reply may be that is exactly the reason why I believe you need this product. The boomerang method is effective only in the hands of the experienced and skilled salesman.

**4. Compensation Method**: This method is similar to that of indirect method as discussed earlier except that here the salesman admits the validity of the objection but offsets the objection by a superior point of greater advantage to the customer. For instance, a customer for a shirt-piece might object that the cloth of the shirt does not seem to be of the best quality. By using this method, the salesman would reply. 'Sir you are quite correct. The cloth is not of the best quality. If it had been, the price would have been considerably higher. The lower price compensates the lower quality'.

**5. Question Method** : In case any customer has raised any question then it becomes natural on the part of the salesman to answer that question. In this case the objection is raised by the customer. Instead of replying to that objection, the salesman asks certain questions from the customer which makes the customer to answer his own objection. For instance, the customer says, "I like this pair of shoes but I cannot purchase the same as it is costly". By using this method, the salesman would say, 'Mr. Customer, why you are wearing such a costly suit? Do you like it? Does it add to your personality? The customer replies, "I wear this suit very much. It has added to my personality. I had paid Rs.5,000 for it," The salesman says, "Why do you not try a suit made by another firm which would cost you only Rs.2,000.? The customer replies, "I always purchase the best quality." Salesman says, "Sir, it is exactly the same with the pair of shoes at a lower price but you neither like it nor it will add to your personality. Further, this pair of shoes would prove more economical in the long run.

**6. Pass-up Method** : Under this method the salesman attempts to smile and pass off many objections. Sometimes salesman pretends not to have heard the objection and passes on to the next point. This method should be used only when the customer has raised a flimsy objection.

**7. Reverse Position Method**: This method is applied in cases where the customer is raising objections one by one which are not based on sound footing. Under this method, the salesman may ask the customer to explain in greater detail his particular objection instead of answering it himself. The background of using this method is that the customer while explaining his objection in detail might himself realize its timeliness. For instance, the customer says, "It is not a good book. While using this method, the salesman would say, "Sir, you seem to know too much about this subject and I am really interested to know more on this subject. Would you please let me know the reasons in detail as to why you do no like this book." The customer would feel ashamed of what he has said earlier. The success of this method depends on the sincerity of the salesman while making the statement and the patience and eagerness he shows to learn reasons behind the customer's statement.

## CLOSING A SALE

Closing a sale is a very important and final part of the selling process. Closing the sale is making the customer say 'yes' to your preparation. The whole object of the entire selling process is to induce the buying decision of the prospect and thereby close the sale. Unless the salesman gets the prospect to agree to buy the product, the entire efforts are wasted. In this way, the objective of closing a sale is to get the customer in a mood of saying 'yes' so that the salesman can ask for the order. The experienced and skilled salesmen know the time when to close a sale and the way to close a sale.

### Method of Closing a Sale

There may be several methods, which may be used for closing a sale by the salesman. The popular methods, as usually used in practice are as follows:

**1. Affirmative Close:** Under this method, the salesman gets the customer to agree to a number of questions. Answers in the affirmative to a few initial questions leave the customer with no other alternative except giving answers in 'yes' to the subsequent questions and thereby leading to a successful close of sale. It should, however, be kept in mind that this method has equal chances of both success and failure and the salesman should be prepared for it. This method although used on many customers seems to be best suited to the talkative and responsive customers.

**2. Erecting Barriers**: Under the method, barriers are erected before the customer closes the sale. Erecting barriers in a sale's close makes it extremely difficult for the customer to escape from buying. For instance, the salesman feels that the customer has almost approved the product but is hesitant in placing the order immediately. The salesman says, "Sir, the offer at the old price of Rs.150 is open for today only. Next day you will have to pay Rs.175 as per the revised price list". No doubt, this of course amounts to high pressure selling but can be used legitimately in many cases successfully. This method is best suited to the silent, unresponsive and non-committal type of customers.

**3. Narrowing the Choice**: Under this method, the salesman closes the sale by narrowing down the choice of the customer. When a customer is offered wide range of product, it becomes difficult for him to reach a decision. Hence the salesman removes all those varieties one by one, in which the customer has shown the least interest. In this way only two or three varieties of a product are left with the customer, which seem to be most suitable and favoured. In this way the sales comes to a close soon.

**4. Offering Inducements**: Under this method, the salesman offers some extra inducements to the customer. Thus a salesman might offer certain concession or special consideration to the customer who may purchase the same in the expectation of extra gains. For instance, the salesman says to the customer, "If you will take the delivery of this case within a fortnight, I shall allow you 5% extra discount".

**5. The Assumption Close**: This method is based on the assumption that the customer has already decided and is going to purchase soon. Under this method, after receiving a positive signal from the customer, the salesman asks the customer to fill in his name overshoot or there may be a shortfall, both of which are detrimental to a sales talk close.

**6. Use Appropriate Timing:** Although the opportunity for closing the sales talk will arise more than once during the interview with the prospect, the salesman must use appropriate timing. As the interview proceeds, the prospect's interest keeps increasing until it reaches a peak. This would be the best time for moving towards the close of the sales talk. For example, when the prospect enquires about the time required for delivery of goods, it is an indication that the prospect has almost decided to purchase the product.

**7. The Test of a Good Sales Talk lies in its Deliver**: All the good points of the product need not be presented simultaneously. They should be presented one by one. After delivering each point the salesman should wait for the reactions of the prospect, reserving always his best point to the last, which must be made use of at the optimum point of the rise in the prospect's interest.

**8. Maintain a Positive Attitude**: The salesman should maintain a positive attitude throughout the sales talk. Hesitancy is the greatest enemy of the salesman. The salesman should always show a calm attitude and hide his tension. He must remain hopeful and should not show his worry about closing the sales talk. The sales talk will materialize with a successful close.

## REVIEW QUESTIONS

1. What do you mean by a selling process?
2. What is prospecting?
3. What is meant by pre-approach?
4. What is sales presentation?
5. What do you mean by dramatization?
6. Explain various steps in selling process
7. Explain the characteristics of a good prospecting.
8. Elucidate the methods of prospecting.
9. Explain various methods of making an approach
10. Explain the essentials of effective sales presentation
11. Explain the methods of handling objections
12. State the methods of closing a sale.

# 8 Sales Talks

## MEANING OF SALES TALKS

Sales talk is the heart of salesmanship. When the salesman and the customer meet and a sales dialogue takes place, it is called sales talk. In other words, any talk between the salesman and the customer intended to sell a product to the buyer is called 'sales talk'. It is one of the outcome of this talk that a sale is either effected or lost. Thus the sale of a product depends on the success of the sales talk. A successful sales talk is a process with a right beginning and right closing. The sales talk must be thoroughly planned and complete in all respects. It should be neither too lengthy nor too short.

## ESSENTIALS OF EFFECTIVE SALES TALKS

A Sales Talk to be effective should have the following essentials or Characteristics

1. **Well Planned:** An effective sales talk is one, which is thoroughly well planned and prepared for the occasion. Planning should be done on both sides, i.e. the salesman and the prospect. Then only it might give desired results.
2. **Courteous and Friendly Atmosphere**: The sales talk should start, proceed and close in a most courteous and friendly atmosphere. Neither salesman nor customer should try to impose his superiority or dominance over the other.
3. **Just and Fair**: The sales talk should be just and fair from the point of view of both the salesman and the customer. A sales talk should not aim at exploiting the customer. There should not be any fraud, misrepresentation or suppressing of facts from the side of salesman.
4. **Confidence:** The sales talk should be such which can create confidence in each other. In case, the salesman has no confidence in the address in the prescribed form he put his signature as a token of confirmation of order. Retailers mostly use this method.
5. **The Pros and Cons Method**: Under this method, the salesman lists all the advantages that will result from the purchase on one side and all the disadvantages, which may appear to the customer on the other side. Afterwards, the salesman proceeds to prove that the advantages out weigh the supposed disadvantages. This method is quite popular these days.
6. **Summarization of the Sales Points:** Under this method the salesman summarises all the selling points and reminds the customer of the reasons at to why he should purchase the product. This should be done in an informal way. Thus when the salesman presents a long list of product's features it becomes difficult for the customer to say 'no' to the salesman.

7. **Implying that a Sales is Made**: Under this method, the salesman replies by words and actions that the customer has made up his mind to purchase the product. If the customer does not stop him, the salesman concludes that everything is 'O, K'. For instance, the salesman presents a book before the customer. The customer turns some pages of the book and keeps it on the table of the salesman. The salesman orders his assistant to pack the book and hand over the same to the customer. The customer does not object. It implies that the sale is closed. This method is widely used these days.
8. **The Direct Close**: It is the most simple and common method of closing a sale. Instead of beating about the bush, the salesman directly asks the customer to place the order to him. The sale is closed as soon as the order is placed.

## THE IMPORTANCE OF CLOSING A SALES TALK

**Sales Close is the Test of a Salesman's Ability to Sell**: Closing sales is the last step in a sales talk. Closing the sale is making the prospect say 'yes' to your proposition. It is like the matter of getting married. Closing is the action on the part of the salesman of concluding the sales transaction. Closing means asking for an order. After the salesman has established rapport with the prospect, demonstrated the product features and benefits, and handled objections if any, he should ask for the order. Unless the salesman gets the order to buy the product, the entire efforts are wasted. Thus, a successful sales talk close is the test of a salesman's ability to sell the product.

**Advantages**

1. **Adds to the Income of the Salesman:** A successful sales talk close brings an added income to the salesman. Most of the business firms pay commission on the sales effected by the salesman besides his monthly salary etc.
2. **Develops Confidence in Salesman:** The successful sales talk closing develops confidence in the salesman, particularly new salesman. If the salesman finds that he is not able to close the sales talk successfully, he loses his enthusiasm, courage and confidence. Thus, an unsuccessful sales talk close results in a salesman feeling diffident and dejected with his work.
3. **Sign of Success of Selling Plan** : Closing the sales talk means securing a favourable reply from the prospect to your selling plan. As a matter of fact, it is the logical conclusion to a satisfactory completion of the selling plan. It is the sign of success of selling plan.
4. **End of Tension**: So long the sales talk is not concluded both the salesman and the prospect remain under tension. However, the salesman is likely to get more tense. The tension comes to close (end) as soon as the sales talk is closed. Both the salesman and the prospect feel at ease as soon as the sales talk comes to an end successfully.

## SALES MEETINGS, CONFERENCES AND CONVENTIONS:

### Meaning of Sales Meetings, Conferences and Conventions

According to K.B.Hass, "A sales conference is an open discussion type of meeting of people with similar experience and comparable rank,. directed by a attained conference leader, for the purpose of solving problems through the exchange of ideas." Thus, sales conference or /sales meetings is a meeting of salesmen and their executives which provide occasion for oral interchange of information, ideas and viewpoints to get understanding and acceptance of the solution to common problems. The difference between a sales conference or sales meeting and a sales convention is one of degree rather than of kind. A conference is a meeting called for the purpose of solving common problems through the mutual exchange of information, ideas and viewpoints. It is purely a business type meeting. It can be called monthly, half yearly, yearly or at any time. Conferences or meetings are organsied at some definite specific place. On the other hand, a sales convention is called mainly for promoting social contacts, giving publicity to the products, arranging programmes of entertainment and has the element of education and inspiration. It is in the form of an annual general meeting. It can be held at any place, such as any hill station like Srinagar, Simla or places of historical importance like Agra etc. Thus sales conferences and conventions are important both for employee and the sales personnel.

**Advantages**

1. It provides a platform for mutual exchange of opinions, ideas and view points between the sales executives and the sales force.
2. Salesmen can have the opportunity of coming in close contact with the senior and experienced sales executives. It enhances their knowledge.
3. Such meetings develop love, affection, mutual cooperation and team spirit amongst the members. Misunderstanding, if any, may be removed on the spot.
4. It increases the efficiency, knowledge, morale and self confidence of the participants.
5. Discussions also disclose the shortcomings, handicaps and weakness of the sales organization. The sales manager can take necessary corrective steps to remove them in due course of time.
6. Such conferences and conventions develop a sense of responsibility, pride and loyalty amongst the salesmen towards the enterprise.
7. They provide requisite information and knowledge about the sales policy, sales targets, strategy, sales promotion activities, new products, latest techniques of facing competition and the progress of the enterprise.
8. Prizes are also awarded to the sales force on the basis of their performances. It provides the inspiration to the other salesmen.
9. Sales conferences and conventions provide an opportunity to every salesman for self-evaluation.
10. Organizing such sales conferences and conventions is a symptom of progressive sales management. It increases the goodwill of the enterprise.

**Disadvantages**

1. Organizing sales conferences and conventions is an expensive job. Only large enterprises can afford it.
2. Sales activities during the course of such conferences and conventions remain closed.
3. The routine activities of the enterprise are adversely affected.
4. Sometimes the outspoken sales personnel misuse these sales conferences and conventions. Groups are formed and drug of war takes place.
5. It is a time-consuming process.

## Sales Contest

### Meanings

Sales contests are taken as one of the measures of sales promotion. According to Still and Cundiff, "A sales contest is a special selling campaign offering salesmen incentives in the form of prizes or awards above and beyond those provided by the compensation plan." Sales contests are most popular with firms specializing in consumer products like food and drugs etc. The main object of sales contests is to provide sales personnel with extra incentives to increase sales volume and also bring more profits to the company. According to Herzberg "Sales contests aim at fulfilling the needs of individuals for achievement and recognition." If they are well-organised, they can be used to counter 'off-season' decline in sales and bring in new customers. They also generate team spirit among the salesmen and foster a sense of cooperation. These sales contests bring out the talented and more intelligent salesmen to the forefront.

### Objectives of the Sales Contests

Sales contests motivate salesmen to increase sales volume along with higher profits. The main objectives of sales contests are as follows:

1. To increase overall sales.
2. To attract new customers
3. To arrest seasonal sales slumps
4. To push new products, high margin goods and slow moving goods
5. To get repeated orders from present and former customers
6. To improve sales personnel performance
7. To bring a spirit of competition among the salesmen
8. To improve customer's services
9. To achieve the sales targets
10. To increase incentives to sales force
11. To popularize the products of the company
12. To bring talented and intelligent salesmen to the forefront
13. To generate team spirit among the salesmen and foster a sense of cooperation.

### Precautions for Planning Sales contests

Sales contests, if at all they are to be a success, must be properly planned by the sales manager. In this connection the following precautions should be kept in mind before finalizing any scheme of sales contests:

1. The purpose or result aimed at should be very clearly defined and published.
2. Conditions, rules and regulations etc. should be quite simple and easily understandable by all.
3. The time and date of the sales contests should be chosen with great care.
4. The sales contests should be such in which everybody can participate and have equal chances of winning the prizes etc.
5. Interest of the participants should be maintained throughout the contest.
6. Both the employer and the sales force must be benefited by the sales contest.
7. The sales contest must motivate the sales force to expand increased efforts.

8. Extra prizes should be given for the 'first order', 'the biggest order', 'the greatest number of orders' and so on.
9. Prizes that may have a permanent value, such as watches, cycles, scooters, books etc. should be given so that they may keep a salesman enthusiastic after the contest.
10. The members of the contest committee should be impartial and acceptable to sales personnel.

**Advantages of Sales contests**

The main advantages of sales contests are as follows:

1. The sales contests increase the sales volume along with increase in profits of the company.
2. Sales contests stimulate salesman's efforts more vigorously to attain the sales targets.
3. The possibility of winning the prizes attracts young, talented and efficient salesmen to offer their services more effectively.
4. During slump period, sales contests are the best means of not only arresting the decline in sales but also raising the volume of sales.
5. Sales contests generate team spirit among the salesmen and foster a sense of cooperation.
6. The sales contests are helpful in bringing out the talented and more intelligent salesmen to the forefront for promotion purposes.
7. Sales contests raise the morale of the sales force and develop the spirit of competition.
8. Sales contests increase the goodwill and the reputation of the company.
9. New customers are attracted on account of sales contests.
10. Consumers are also benefited by sales contests.

**Disadvantages, Limitations or Objections of Sales contests**

The disadvantages, limitations or objections of sales contests are as follows:

1. Sales contests do not really increase sales over the long run, but they merely provide a short-term sales expansion.
2. High caliber and more experienced sales personnel look upon the sales contests as juvenile and silly.
3. Sales contests cause sales personnel to launch their sales efforts during the competition and thus sales slump occurs both before and after the sales contests.
4. The disappointment suffered by sales contests losers causes a general decline in sales force morale and enthusiasm.
5. Sales contests distract salesmen from the main job of selling and encourage them only to concentrate on winning prizes by fair or foul means.
6. Sales contests lead to unanticipated and undesirable results, such as, increased returns and adjustments, higher credit losses and overstocking by dealers.
7. Sales contests are temporary devices for motivating sales force, and if used too frequently, have a narcotic effect. No greater results in the aggregate are obtained with such contests.

8. When the product is in short supply, it is ridiculous to organize sales contests.
9. It is argued that the sales force is regularly paid for their services under the basic compensation plan. Hence there is no necessity of organizing sales contests.
10. According to Still and Cundiff, "The competition atmosphere generated by sales contest weakens team spirit".

### Do Sales contests Motivate?

In view of the above objections and criticisms, it is generally argued whether the sales contests really motivate the sales force to increase sales and profits of the company, In this connection it may be said that in spite of these objections, limitations and criticisms, sales contests are widely used by most of the companies in and outside the country. Their popularity is increasing day by day. Sales contests are the source of motivation to the sales personnel. They provide recognition, excitement and reward to sales force. It provides new excitement and challenge to the sales force.

There are four forms/kinds of sales contests prizes:

1. Cash prizes
2. Merchandise prizes
3. Travel and
4. Special Honour or Privileges

1. **Cash prizes**: Sales contest prize in the form of cash is quite popular and is considered to be an important motivating factor. However, this amount in the form of cash prize must be substantial so as to motivate the salesman as he is already getting a handsome salary from the company.
2. **Merchandise prizes**: The merchandise prize is considered superior as compared to the cash prize in several respects. For instance, winners of the merchandise prize have permanent evidence of their achievement. The monetary value of the merchandise prize is also generally higher than the cash prize. The merchandize prize is usually of permanent nature.

   However, to make the scheme more effective, merchandise prizes must be selected carefully. It will be better if the winners are alowed to select their own prizes from a variety of offerings.
3. **Travel:** In modern times, travel awards are gaining popularity, particularly among young salesmen. Young and energetic salesmen are tempted by travel awards to places of luxury report. To make the award more attractive, generally, trips for both the winners and their spouses are offered by the company.
4. **Special Honours and Privileges**: Special honours and privileges are inexpensive and provide a strong incentive to the sales force. It may take the form of an appreciation letter issued by the top executive (such as general manager or managing director) of the company, membership of a special club or association that enjoys certain privileges, trophies, publicity in leading newspapers etc. This type of award fulfils the esteem and self-actualization needs of the sales force.

### Essentials for the success of Sales conferences and conventions

The following points should be kept in mind for the success of sales conferences and conventions:

(*i*) At least 30 days prior notice should be given to the participants with the date, time, place and the agenda to the participants.

(*ii*) The agenda of the meeting should be well-planned, exhaustive and interesting so as to enable the participants to participate and keep them busy. It should be circulated well in advance.

(*iii*) The sales conferences and conventions should provide an atmosphere of free and open discussions to the participants. Nobody should be allowed to thrust his opinion over others. The members should be allowed to criticise the policies and also forward useful suggestions.

(*iv*) Proper arrangements should be made as to stay, food, recreation, and transport of the participants.

(*v*) The senior, experienced and influential person of the sales organization should convene sales conferences and conventions. They should be conducted in accordance with the agenda duly circulated amongst the participants well in advance.

(*vi*) It should be kept in mind that the ultimate object of organizing sales conferences and conventions is to stimulate the sales force so as to discharge their duties more efficiently.

(*vii*) Necessary evaluation is done by the sales management in time. The evaluation should be based on as to what extent the aims of conference and convention are accomplished. To accomplish this, feedback from the participants is necessary.

## REVIEW QUESTIONS

1. What is a Sales Talk?
2. What is a Sales Conference?
3. What is a Sales Contest?
4. What is a Sales Convention?
5. State the Essentials of a Sales Talk
6. State the merits and demerits of Sales conferences
7. What are the objectives of a Sales Contest?
8. What are the merits and demerits of Sales contests.
9. State the importance of closing a salestalk.
10. What are sales meetings?
11. State the precautian for planning a sales contest.
12. Bring out the essentials for success of sales conferences and convention.

# 9 Functions of Sales Manager

The functions/duties of a sales manager are many and varied. They may be classified under the following three heads:

1. Managerial/executive duties or functions
2. Administrative duties or functions
3. Miscellaneous duties or functions

## (1) MANAGERIAL / EXECUTIVE DUTIES OR FUNCTIONS

The main function of the sales manager is the management of sales operations including sales programmes and sales personnel. The management of sales programmes includes establishment and developing short-term and long-term sales policies and sales objectives, in consultation with other heads of related departments. He develops detailed sales programmes for his department designed to improve competitive positions, to minimize re-distribution costs and to achieve pre-determined sales goals in terms of amount and quantity. For this purpose he should review and approve and, if necessary, improve sales strategies, sales policies, sales objectives and pricing policies of the respective products.

The management of sales personnel function includes recruitment, selection, training, direction, supervision, motivation and control of sales personnel in the best interest of the organization. In smaller organizations, the top executive of the sales department, i.e. sales manager himself, performs this function. However, in large organizations, services of staff specialists are made useful. He fixes sales territory and sales quota for every salesman, watches his performance and takes necessary timely action to correct his performance. The sales manager is also a link between salesmen and top management just to communicate the market needs to the top management and the wishes of the top management to the salesmen.

## (2) ADMINISTRATIVE FUNCTIONS

Sales manager is the administrative head of sales department having full control over the staff of the department and administering the sales office. He establishes an effective plan of sales organization and also controls the activities of the entire sales staff working under his control. He is the leader of the sales personnel at all levels and guides, directs and provides them proper incentive so as to perform their duties effectively.

Administration of sales office is one of the important functions of the sales manger. It involves considerable amount of paper work and record-keeping, depending on the nature of activities assigned to sales department.

### (3) MISCELLANEOUS FUNCTIONS

(1) Maintenance of cordial and effective relationship with the heads of other departments within the company.

(2) To ensure that long-term customer relationship is maintained so as to achieve the goals of the enterprise

(3) To conduct selling personally so as to increase the sales volume. For this purpose he plans, develops and implements the field sales strategy, supervises the sales personnel and coordinates and controls the sales efforts of sales personnel.

(4) To study the market conditions, problems of competition and the substitutes coming into the market. He is required to inform the top management of these facts along with his suggestions

(5) To maintain discipline in the sales organization.

(6) To organize activities relating to sales promotion, such as, contests, seminars, conferences and provide incentives to the sales staff and the customers.

(7) To plan and organize distribution channel in consultation with top management

(8) To analyze the market thoroughly from time to time.

(9) To undertake advertising campaign keeping in view the cost and sales requirements.

(10) To plan sales targets in consultation with other departments, such as, production department

(11) To prepare sales budget of a given period.

Thus, the sales manager performs a number of functions depending on the nature of products and the size of the enterprise.

## RESPONSIBILITIES OF SALES MANAGER

According to A.L. Reid, the responsibilities of a manager can be grouped under Fire heads, i.e.

(1) Responsibility to himself

(2) Responsibility towards organization

(3) Responsibility towards customers.

(4) Responsibilities towards his staff and

(5) Miscellaneous.

They may be studied as under:

### (1) Responsibility to self

The foremost responsibility of the sales manager is to make him competent for the work assigned to him by the enterprise. In this connection he must evaluate himself from time to time and make necessary improvements accordingly. According to A.L.Reid the following are the responsibilities towards himself :

(*i*) To increase managerial abilities.

(*ii*) To increase and develop selling abilities

(*iii*) To keep himself in contact with regional changes and developments

(*iv*) To have knowledge of latest marketing techniques.

(*v*) To have detailed knowledge of the products

(*vi*) To make continuous and sincere efforts for removing his weaknesses.

(*vii*) To develop the spirit of cooperation, possess progressive outlook and have good temperament.

**(2) Responsibility towards Organization**

Since Sales Manager is a vital part of the entire organization, he has a number of responsibilities towards the organization. They may be summarized as under :

1. To maintain and also increase the goodwill of the enterprise among his customers
2. To prepare the records and reports etc. of his department regularly and present the same before the top management accordingly.
3. To take steps of reducing sales cost.
4. To keep a constant watch on the activities of the competitors and keep the top management aware of them along with his suggestions.
5. To make sincere efforts at achieving sales targets.
6. To coordinate and cooperate with the other departments.
7. To feel proud of the organization
8. To keep the organization in touch with the changes that are taking place in his region, department etc.
9. To seek and also provide assistance and cooperation to the enterprise as and when required. To maintain true and complete accounts of his department.

**(3) Responsibility towards Customers**

1. To remain in constant touch with the customers through sales promotion and advertisement
2. To explain to the customers the advantages that they can have by keeping themselves in touch with the company.
3. To provide information to the customers about the miscellaneous uses of the products.
4. To keep himself in touch particularly with those salesmen who command influence on customers.
5. To take interest and listen to the complaints of the customers and make sincere efforts for solving the same satisfactorily.

**(4) Responsibility Towards Salesmen**

1. To explain the technique of presenting the products in such a way before the customers which is less time consuming, cheaper and more effective.
2. To recruit, select, train, supervise, control, remunerate, motivate and promote the sales force so that it may perform the duties more efficiently and effectively.
3. To explain the methods of dealing with the customer's' complaints effectively.
4. To provide the detailed knowledge about the products.
5. To arrange and plan salesmen's tours, allocate sales territories, fix sales quotas of each salesman and check the compliance from time to time.
6. To listen and remove the grievances, complaints and problems of the sales force and take necessary timely steps for solving the same. He must see that no clash of interest takes place.

**(5) Miscellaneous**

(i) Responsibility as to maintenance of public relations

(ii) Responsibility as to office management

(iii) Responsibility as to sales planning, sales targets, sales policies, sales forecasting, sales research etc

(iv) Responsibility as to reducing sales costs in view of sales volume.

(v) Responsibility as to collect and analyse statistics in connection with marketing research, product research and consumer research etc.

## RELATIONS OF SALES MANAGER WITH TOP MANAGEMENT AND OTHERS

Ordinarily there are three levels of management i.e Top Management, Middle Management and Lower Management. The overall control of the enterprise lies in the hands of the Top Management. The success of the sales manager/sales executive depends very much on the cordial relations with top management. He should strive for personal goals as well as for organizational goals, but to achieve both these goals it is essential on his progress made in both these directions. Likewise, for successful achievement of sales department objectives, harmonious relations, proper communication and exchange of views are necessary. Any sort of misunderstanding is liable to do severe harm to the enterprise as a whole.

Since sales manager is the head of sales organization, he is responsible for all the activities relating to his department to the top management. He should plan his organizational goals in coordination with enterprise goals. Now to achieve his goals he should formulate plans. Now before implementing his plans he is expected to inform the top management about his goals and seek necessary advice and guidance, if any. These goals cannot be achieved without the help of top management. More often, the sales manager should consult the top management before taking any policy decision. It is essential that his policy decision should be strictly in accordance with the overall policy of the enterprise, which is framed exclusively by the top management. Any deviation from the overall enterprise policy will not only damages their relationship but also will amount to gross violation of the authority entrusted to him by the top management.

## REVIEW QUESTIONS

1. State the main functions of a Sales Manager
2. What is administration of Sales Office?
3. List out the various levels of management.
4. State the Managerial functions of a Sales Manager
5. State the responsibilities of a Sales Manager towards organization.

# 10 Recruitment and Selection of Salesmen

## SOURCES OF RECRUITMENT OF SALESMEN

The recruitment of salesmen is important not only in the formation of a new sales force, but also in the successful operation of an established organization. The sources of recruitment of salesmen can be classified under two heads: They are

1. Internal Sources of Recruitment
2. External Sources of Recruitment

### 1. INTERNAL SOURCES OF RECRUITMENT:

It means recruiting the salesman amongst the workers already working in the enterprise. In other words it means recruitment within the organization. The main internal sources of recruitment of a salesman are as follows.

#### (1) Present Employees Already Working in the Organization

Recruitment may be done from the inside staff working in different departments. This is perhaps the safest and most profitable method. A person recruited from the inside staff would generally possess some knowledge of the product as well as the principles and general policy of the enterprise in which he is working. He may even be familiar with the customers of the enterprise and thus a readymade salesman may be recruited from inside the staff itself.

#### (2) Recommendation of the Existing Salesman

Salesman may also be recruited on the basis of recommendation of the existing salesman already working in the organization. The advantage of this method is that the salesman already working in the organization knows the requirements of the job in question and hence he would be in a position to make a suitable recommendation. They may include ex-salesman, other workers, relatives, sons and daughters of the salesman etc. It increases the loyalty of the employees towards the enterprise.

#### (3) Promotions

As a matter of policy, firms employ sales personnel from within by promoting the employees from lower post to higher post. It is a good step because the person who has put in service feels recognized and puts forth his best on his promotion. Thus it is also an important internal source of recruitment.

#### (4) Transfers

Particularly in large-sized organizations, transfer of employees from one department to another department is a normal feature. Hence employees of the firms other departments and non-selling section of the sales department may also be considered for careers in sales department. The personnel department has the history of each employee working in the enterprise and thereby the chance of potentially promoting one can be considered by transfers.

### (5) Re-employment of Former Employees

It is another important internal source of recruitment. In case of those ex-workers whose past record is clean and sound may be called back to their original work situations provided they are willing and both mentally as well as physically sound to take up the job with loyalty and sincerity.

## MERITS OR ADVANTAGES OF INTERNAL SOURCE OF RECRUITMENT

(*i*) The loyalty and cooperation of the staff are increased.

(*ii*) The training period is minimized.

(*iii*) The break-in period is reduced. He can easily be adjusted to the new environment.

(*iv*) Generally a person recruited from within the enterprise need not be paid very high remuneration.

(*v*) It has already been proved that where a much specialised knowledge of a highly technical product is necessary, inside staff has proved to be the best.

(*vi*) Employee's morale is increased and they also feel motivated.

(*vii*) The efficiency and conduct of such persons can be easily evaluated.

(*viii*) Sales manager usually prefers a man coming from within the organization.

## DEMERITS OR DISADVANTAGES OF INTERNAL SOURCE OF RECRUITMENT

(*i*) Jealousy and dissatisfaction develop among the workers who are not recruited

(*ii*) A kind of monopoly of the workers is established. They will tend to claim as their personal right and privilege, to be considered and recruited for the job in question

(*iii*) It is said that the old workers usually lack enthusiasm. They usually oppose any change.

(*iv*) Since the field of recruitment is limited it might not be easy to get the right man having requisite qualifications and experience etc.

(*v*) Salesmen recruited from competitors may also bring new customers with them. But the same is not the case with a person recruited from within the organization.

(*vi*) It must be remembered that the inside employee is a hot-house plant, nurtured within the working of the sales organization. If he is called upon to work on a job of different nature, it may not be a success, such as the work of a traveling salesman.

(*vii*) This injects heavy doses of stagnation and inefficiency. Once a person gets his position easily, he becomes complacent and lethargic because he has achieved a height which he does not deserve.

## 2. EXTERNAL SOURCES OF RECRUITMENT :

The main external sources of recruitment of salesman are as follows:

1. Through advertisement in newspapers.

2. Competitor's staff members
3. Schools and Colleges
4. Employment Exchanges
5. Voluntary Applications
6. Recommendations of Customers
7. Relatives and Friends
8. Employment Seekers

## MERITS OR ADVANTAGES OF EXTERNAL SOURCES OF RECRUITMENT

(1) More efficient, skilled and educated persons can be recruited as suited to the job
(2) Jealousy and dissatisfaction among the existing workers is avoided
(3) New person also brings new ideas, new techniques with himself.
(4) Recruitment from external sources is based on merits and hence such a person is expected to give better performance.
(5) It is easy for the sales manager to bring necessary changes as per his choice.
(6) Control and supervision work becomes comparatively easy
(7) He also brings new customers
(8) If found unsuitable, the services can be easily terminated.

## DE-MERITS OR DISADVANTAGES OF EXTERNAL SOURCES OF RECRUITMENT

(1) Loyalty and Cooperation among the workers is reduced.
(2) Training becomes expensive and time consuming
(3) Frustration develops if promotion is not given after due period, say 5 to 10 years.
(4) It takes a long time in understanding the working and the policies of the organization and getting himself adjusted in the new environment
(5) The post remains vacant from the date of selection up to the date of joining the enterprise. Thus the working of the enterprise suffers.

## CONSIDERATIONS TO BE MADE FOR THE SELECTION OF SALESMEN

Since the work of a salesman is of varied nature, it is difficult to lay out the definite principles or points or consideration for the selection of a salesman. In general, the following principles or points should be kept in mind while selecting the salesman.

1. He must have aptitude for salesmanship. This can be judged at the time of interview and the past record of the candidate.
2. He must be educated and possess sufficient knowledge of language. He should have knowledge preferably of three languages i.e. English, Hindi and local language of the field in which he is to be appointed.
3. The age of the candidate to be selected should be preferably between 22 years to 30 years.
4. The candidate should be physically and mentally fit for the job of salesman.
5. The candidate to be selected for the job should have good nature and temperament so that he can influence the customers.
6. The candidate must have good habits. A drunkard, gambler and corrupt person are liable to ruin the business of the enterprise.

7. He must have a strong character
8. He should have adequate knowledge of human psychology.
9. Absence of pride.
10. As far as possible, the candidate should have adequate experience of salesmanship in a reputed concern.
11. In case the enterprise deals in technical products such as machinery, then the candidate should have adequate technical knowledge so that he could give a good demonstration of the product before the prospective customers.

## SCIENTIFIC PROCESS OF SELECTION OF SALESMEN

It is difficult to prescribe one selection procedure for the salesman, which may be sued in all the enterprises. The selection procedure used will differ, depending upon a number of factors, such as the nature of the product, size of sales organization, marketing environment, existence of competition, promotional programmes adopted by the competitors, size of the market, i.e. local, national or international, size of the enterprise and finally number and nature of customers. A wise selection procedure ensures an effective sales force. Consequently there would be an increase in the sales per salesman and better customer relations. However, in general, the ideal or scientific sales process should include the following:

(1) Job Analysis, Job Description and Man Specification
(2) Source of Selection-Advertisement
(3) Application Form
(4) Personal Interview
(5) References: Investigation or Checking
(6) Psychological Tests
(7) Medical Examination
(8) Final Interview and Selection

**Selection Process**

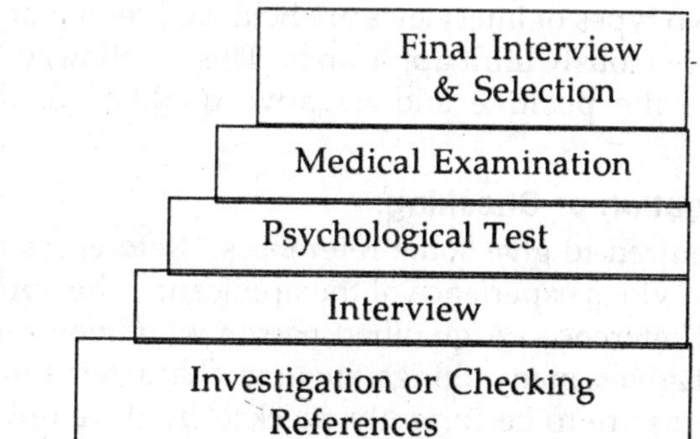


### (1) Job Analysis, Job Description and Man Specification

A good job analysis helps not only in connection with selection of salesmen but also in the evaluation, supervision, training and compensation payable to a salesman. Job description gives the requirements of the particular job. On the contrary, man specification gives the details of qualities and qualifications etc. which are required in the salesman. In this way, the starting point of selection process is job analysis, job description and man specification which should be decided in advance.

**(2) Source of Selection – Advertisement:**

As already discussed in the earlier question there are a number of sources of selection of salesman depending on a number of factors. However, the most common source of selection as used by most of the enterprises is the advertisement. The advertisement should clearly state the nature of the business and the qualification required of the applicants in question. Further, the advertisement may be open or closed. Open advertisement includes the name and address of the employers. On the contrary, closed advertisement simply bears the Post Box No... and not the name and address of the employer. However, closed advertisement should be preferred so as to have genuine selection. Further, the advertisement should be given in a leading newspaper, such as Hindustan Times or Times of India etc.

**(3) Application Form:**

Most of the employers have their own printed blank application forms. The blank application forms, besides other things, contain a list of questions, which the applicant is required to answer. The questions relate to those qualities and the information, which are considered essential by the employer for the job in question. The advantages of this system are that the applications are standardized providing an automatic test of intelligence, accuracy, neatness and thoroughness. These blank application forms are either supplied free of cost or on minor fees to the applicants. The application form duly filled by the applicant must reach the company's office in time as given in the advertisement. The applicant is also required to give references.

**(4) Personal Interview :**

This is the most important stage of selection procedure. Interviews have a dual purpose (i) to determine the applicant's fitness for the sales job, and (ii) to present the job to applicants. In the interview the sales manager forms his opinion of the applicant's appearance, voice, poise, bearing, resourcefulness, hobbies, taste, intelligence and capability etc. Usually, two types of interviews are held, i.e preliminary interview is held for screening quickly the obviously unfit applicants. This is followed by comprehensive or final interview where the positive and negative qualities of the applicants are weighted carefully.

**(5) References: Investigation or Checking:**

The applicant is required to give some references. References may be relative to character, education or previous experience of the applicant. The applicant may also be required to give personal reference. A qualified person who knows the applicant gives a personal reference. It gives many things such as character, integrity etc. of the applicant. These references are to be carefully checked by the employers. If properly handled, references can be of valuable aid to employment since they often disclose important facts which may not otherwise be uncovered.

**(6) Psychological Tests :**

As soon as an applicant qualifies for comprehensive selection, he is required to appear in psychological tests. These psychological tests do help in measuring ability, skill, emotional attitudes, behaviour patterns and aptitude of the applicants. Psychological tests are of various types such as personality test, attitude test, personality test, interest test, general knowledge test etc. These psychological tests may be held according to the level of the post.

**(7) Medical Examination:**

After passing the above tests, the successful applicants are required to appear before the duly constituted medical board for medical examination. The object of medical examination is to select those persons who are physically fit for the job of the salesmen.

**(8) Final Interview and Selection:**

After crossing all the seven hurdles, the candidate stands the chances of final interview and selection. The final interview provides an opportunity to question an applicant further concerning his liabilities and to decide his employment finally. As soon as the applicant is finally selected, he may be requested to report on duty on a stipulated date, time and place as stated in the appointment letter. Before issuing the appointment letter, the organization may like to enter into a contract, putting in writing the conditions of salesman's employment. He may also be asked to give a bond or security etc.

## REVIEW QUESTIONS

1. What are the various sources of recruitment?
2. What is job description?
3. What are psychological tests?
4. State the merits and demerits of external sources of recruitment
5. State the factors to be kept in mind while selecting a salesman
6. Explain the scientific process of selecting salesman.
7. State the merits and demerits of internal sources of recruitment.
8. What are various sources of external recruitment.

# 11 Training of Salesmen

## TRAINING OF SALESMEN

Salesman selected for the job need training for effective sales performance. According to Edwin B. Flippo, "Training is the act of increasing knowledge and skill of an employee for doing a particular job". According to National Society of Sales Training Executives, U.S.A., "Sales training is the intentional and sound application of ordinary human sense to the problem of helping the sales personnel to make the most of its talents". According to George R. Collins, "Sales training is an organized activity involving fact finding, planning, coaching, practice, criticism and accommodation in a purposive attempt to develop selling skills and to add these skills to selected native ability, casually acquired knowledge and experience".

From the above definitions, we conclude that "Sales training is a technique or method by which efforts are made to increase the knowledge, skill and efficiency of a salesman so that he may be in a position to solve the problems of sales and provide active contribution in increasing sales of the enterprise.

## ADVANTAGES OR IMPORTANCE OR ARGUMENTS IN FAVOUR OF SALESMAN'S TRAINING

According to B.R. Canfiled, "Good salesmen are not born but made by properly organized and directed sales training programme". A newly appointed salesman is neither aware of the products nor knows the technique of attracting and presenting the product before the prospective customer. Training makes the salesman aware of all these. In short, the following are the advantages or arguments in favour of training of salesmen:

(*i*) According to Maynard and Davis, "A scientifically designed training programme results in increased sales".

(*ii*) Trained salesmen can see opportunities in a market which have been previously overlooked.

(*iii*) Training is necessary not only to those who are dealing in speciality goods but also to others. A salesman, even though he is a born salesman, requires to be trained in connection to policy and views of the enterprise.

(*iv*) According to Asley and Riso, "Training motivates salesman to remain in the enterprise". He sees better promotion chances and better remuneration in the near future.

(*v*) With increase in sales the cost of selling per unit is reduced considerably.

(*vi*) Training enables salesmen to gain a deeper understanding of the customer's problems and as such can help in solving such problems more efficiently and quickly.

(*vii*) Trained salesman knows his job quite well and therefore needs less supervision and control resulting in a smaller supervision cost.

(*viii*) Trained salesmen acquire deeper insight into customer's needs and wants.

(ix) Properly trained salesman is in a better position to face the keen competition that may exist in the business.

(x) Credit losses are considerably reduced incase of trained salesmen.

(xi) Training helps to lessen the time that a newly selected person takes in picking up his job.

(xii) Training relieves the enterprises of inefficient salesmen who may be a burden on the enterprise.

(xiii) Training helps the salesmen in building congenial relations with customers. A trained salesman is in a position to secure high degree of understanding and cooperation with the customers.

(xiv) Increased volume of business resulting from training is not only advantageous to the enterprise but is also in the interest of the salesmen who may expect better remuneration and promotion etc.

Arguments against Training Salesman or Disadvantages of Training or Limitations of Sales Training

- Some of the experts are of the opinion that "Salesmen are born and not made". Just as a poet or good dancer is born and not made, similarly a good salesman is born. He is gifted with natural qualities of salesmen and hence training is uncalled for.
- Taking into consideration the indefinite results secured, the cost of training is too high. It ranges between Rs. 25,000 to Rs. 65,000 depending on the complexity of the sales job. Particularly small enterprises cannot dare to establish their own training center.
- Tempting offers are made by competitors to trained and good salesman. As such it becomes difficult to retain such salesman. As such the expenditure incurred on the training of a salesman proves to be a waste.
- Training is a means and not an end. It is not essential that a trained salesman may come to the level as required.
- Even admitting that training is necessary the process of training is too slow. The salesman might become impatient and hence it is likely that he may leave the job even before completing the training.
- Salesmanship is a matter of personality and cannot be acquired through training.
- Every salesman has his own way of doing work, and that to impose a system of training upon him will simply spoil his successful methods without eradicating his faults.
- If a person desires to learn swimming, the best way is to get into the water and swim and he will learn, swimming himself. Similar is the case with the training of a salesman. All the theoretical knowledge imparted to a salesman is of no use if not accompanied with practical training.

- Different types of salesmen are recruited for different types of jobs. However, it is not possible to provide all types of training under one roof.
- Some sales managers do not consider training to a salesman desirable as they do not have either sufficient time or required skill and talent to provide training to salesman. They feel that it will adversely affect their duties.
- Most of the employers hesitate to train their sales army because it is time consuming process. In case of a salesman dealing in staple consumer goods a training period of 18 days to 18 months is needed. On the contrary, in the case of specialty and technical products, the period ranges from 3 months to 3 years.

## METHODS OF TRAINING OF SALESMEN

Since the work of salesmen is of varied nature and differs widely from industry to industry, it is not possible to suggest or prescribe any single method of training to salesmen which may suit all types of salesmen. That is why different types of salesmen are appointed for different types of jobs in a sales department. Hence there are different methods of training salesmen. They may be studied under the following two broad heads

1. Individual Training Methods
2. Group Training Methods

### 1. Individual Training Method

The individual training methods include on the job training, training through correspondence, internship training, training through study courses, training through individual coaching, training through special assignments, observation posts etc. as given below.

#### *(i) Training on the Job*

It is a practical method of training in which the trainee gets actual experience by working along with some senior supervisor on the job. It is the most popular method of training. It is also called 'training within industry' or 'coach and pupil training'. Trainees work along with senior supervisor until the senior supervisor is fully satisfied that the trainee is competent to work individually. Under this method of training process charts, manuals, demonstration, tape records etc. are also used.

#### *(ii) Training through Correspondence*

Under this method training is provided to the trainees through correspondence. The special study courses are supplied to the trainees through post by a recognized institution regularly at the residence of the trainees. On the basis of the study courses the trainee is required to answer questions. These answers are duly examined by the panel of the institution regularly. The trainees are intimated about the mistakes committed by them. After a certain period the trainees are required to appear for an informal examination. As soon as they pass the prescribed examination degrees or certificates to the trainees are awarded.

#### *(iii) Internship Training*

This method of training refers to a joint programme of training in which the technical institution and business houses cooperate. The object of such cooperation is to provide theoretical and practical training both side by side to the trainees. As soon as the trainees complete their training they are taken in the regular service of the concerned business house.

### *(iv) Training through Study Courses*

Under this method of training study courses are prepared under the direct supervision and guidance of the experts. Necessary illustration is done through photos and pictures. These study courses are supplied to the trainees who are required to have a detailed study of the same. These study courses are supplied on different intervals. The idea behind this method of training is to refresh the trainee with latest and up-to-date techniques and methods of salesmanship.

### *(v) Training through Individual Coaching*

Under this method of training coaching is provided by the supervisor to the trainees on a continuous and regularly scheduled basis. It is essential that the supervisor should consider the training of the trainee placed under him, as part of this job.

### *(vi) Training through special assignments*

Under this method of training the trainees are provided special assignments with complete freedom to handle the affairs as they please. This method of training aims to create confidence in the trainee to do the task to the best of his ability.

### *(vii) Observation Posts*

This method stresses learning by observation. 'Assistant to' positions make good observation posts in development of the trainee. Trainees holding assistant posts are likely to grasp and assimilate problems pertaining to a particular post most effectively.

## 2. Group Training Method

Under this method training is provided in groups. The advantage of this method is that training is provided to several trainees at a time. The most common methods under group training are as follows:

### *(1) The Lecture Method*

This is the easiest, quickest, simplest and cheapest method of providing training to the trainees. Under this method lectures are delivered by senior supervisors and leading experts to a group of trainees consisting of 15 to 20 trainees who are sitting in a room. This is a sort of classroom lecture method. It is the traditional method of providing training. Visual aids are also used so as to make the lecture most effective. After the lecture, questions are asked so as to have a clear conception. As soon as the desired series of lectures are completed, written and oral examinations may be arranged.

### *(2) The Conference and Seminar Method*

Under this method conferences and seminars are arranged under the leadership of experts and the trainees are required to participate in the same. All those present acquire latest and up to date information on the basis of actual contribution in one way or the other. This method can create greater degree of interest, gives a chance to each one to participate, develops group morale and stimulates analytical thinking.

### *(3) Committee Method*

Under this method committees are formed under the leadership of a senior supervisor. The trainees are the members of the committees. The idea behind this method is to teach the trainees about organizational relationship and help the member (trainee) to visualize the operations of each major organizational unit of the enterprise.

The trainee thus gets wider perspective having to adjust and accommodate others viewpoints and thereby gain practice in reaching decisions.

### *(4) Case Method*

Under this method an actual or hypothetical case of sales is discussed by the trainees in the presence and guidance of a senior supervisor. This method was developed by Harvard Business School of America in 1920-25. There are open and frank discussions amongst the members (trainees).

### *(5) Round Table Method*

Under this method, the trainees are required to sit around a table under the leadership of a senior supervisor or expert. They discuss and express their ideas on a particular subject. It is the best method of having mutual exchange of ideas amongst the trainees on a particular subject.

### *(6) The Panel Method*

Under the panel method, a discussion is presented by a certain number of experts on the panel who take the trouble to prepare and present the facts and discussions. The same further follows with the general discussion in which active participation of the trainees takes place.

### *(7) Role Playing Method*

Under this method training is provided to the trainees by presenting a sales drama before the trainees. In this method a salesman is required to face the problems, criticism and objections of a number of customers. He solves their problems and replies to the criticism and objections in a very skillful, pleasing and convincing manner. It is an interesting and effective method of training.

### (8) Job Rotation Method

Under this method the trainees are required to work on different types of jobs in the sales organization. It provides boarding, balancing and enriching experience to the trainees. However, in order to make this system more effective the number and sequences of the jobs used for training should be carefully selected.

### *(9) The 'Brainstorming' Method*

Under this method any particular problem is thrown at the persons (trainees) sitting round the table and the participants throw out whatever comes into their minds. No one is permitted to contradict. Some good ideas are selected and the rest (useless ideas) find their way into the waste paper basket.

### *(10) The 'each-one-train-one' Method:*

Under this method salesmen are divided into teams of two i.e one of them is an old (experienced) salesman while the other is a new trainee. The old salesman teaches the new one all the techniques which he has acquired through his experience.

### *(11) Miscellaneous Methods*

(*i*) Visual training

(*ii*) Sensitivity training

(*iii*) Multiple table method

(iv) You tell it method and

(v) Task force method etc.

## OBJECTIVES OF SALESMEN'S TRAINING

The objectives of salesmen's training may be varied in nature. They may differ from industry to industry, nature of the products, company policies etc. In general, the objectives of salesmen's training are as follows:

(1) Detailed knowledge of the product

(2) Knowledge of sales policy of the enterprise

(3) Knowledge of the basic principles of selling

(4) Knowledge about the sales organization and the enterprise, including history and the goodwill of the enterprise.

(5) Knowledge about the customers.

(6) Knowledge about the competitors and methods to increase sales in view of the competition.

(7) Method of facing customer's objections, convince the customer and create demand of the product.

(8) Method of meeting, convincing and presenting product information to the customers.

(9) Increase the morale of the salesmen.

(10) Increasing sales of the enterprise.

(11) Method of creating new customers

(12) Knowledge about the method of reporting sales, communication of orders of customers, maintenance of accounts, reimbursement of expenses, display and demonstration of products, preparing daily reports, servicing the customers etc.

(13) Acquaint him with the laws and regulations relating to sale of goods.

(14) Equip the salesman with necessary abilities and techniques to carry on his duties with vigor.

(15) Keep him informed of the prevailing market conditions.

(16) Achieving the sales targets.

(17) Increasing the general efficiency of the salesmen

(18) Preparing the salesmen's force for replacing retiring, incompetent salesmen etc.

## PRINCIPLES OR ESSENTIAL OF GOOD TRAINING PROGRAMME

(a) The scope of the training should be clearly defined

(b) The objective of the training should be clearly defined

(c) The subject matter contents of the training programme should be decided according to the needs of organization and in advance.

(d) Duration, timings and place of training are duly fixed.

(e) Training methods should be determined with great care keeping in view the training objects and the contents of the programme.

(f) Opportunities for diversified experience.

(g) Providing formal and informal training.

(*h*) Proper arrangement for execution of the training programme as per the schedule.

(*i*) Procedure for evaluating the results of the training programme.

(*j*) Training programme should always motivate the trainee to learn and acquire knowledge.

(*k*) The training programme must have the contents of new ideas, latest techniques that are helpful in increasing the knowledge and skill of the trainee.

(*l*) The training programme should be adequate, continuous, convenient and also acceptable to the trainees.

## GOOD SALESMAN'S TRAINING PROGRAMME

The salesmen's training programme of the enterprises depends upon a number of factors such as nature types of products, sales policies, scope of the market to be covered by the salesmen (i.e regional, national, international) etc. That is why different enterprises have different salesmen's training programmes. In general a good salesman's training programme should include the following.

(*i*) History, organizational set-up and goodwill of the enterprise.

(*ii*) Sales policies and sales objectives of the enterprise.

(*iii*) Product information such as characteristics, uses, quality, brand, packing, price, comparison with competitors' product etc.

(*iv*) Information about the competitors along with nature of competition.

(*v*) Information about the customers.

(*vi*) The basic principles of salesmanship

(*vii*) Information about channels of distribution.

(*viii*) Information about matters pertaining to day-to-day work such as preparing report, maintenance of accounts, planning touring progarmmes, reimbursement of expenses, communication of orders of customers, display and demonstration of products, servicing the customers etc.

(*ix*) Knowledge about latest sales techniques such as meeting, convincing and presenting product information to the customer facing customer's objections and complaints, method of closing a sale etc.

(*x*) Customer's satisfaction

(*xi*) Creating new customers.

## REVIEW QUESTIONS

1. What do you mean by Training?
2. Name the methods of training of salesmen
3. What is meant by group training method?
4. What is salesman training?
5. State the arguments in favour of training salesmen
6. State the objectives of salesmen training
7. Explain the essentials of good training programme
8. State the general inclusions in a good salesman's training programme.
9. State the arguments against training of salesmen.

# 12 Remuneration / Compensation of Salesmen

## REMUNERATION TO SALESMEN

No remuneration/compensation plan is said to be satisfactory in absolute terms as it involves conflicting objectives of the pay-masters and pay-receivers. Hence a good or sound remuneration/compensation plan is one that tries to meet the expectations and aspirations of sales force on one hand and overall objectives of the management on the other. It must have direct bearing on the productivity and morale of sales-force.

A sound (good or ideal) remuneration plan from both the salesman's point of view and of the management should have the following essential features, characteristics or principles.

**(1) Simple:** The remuneration plan should be simple, easy to understand and calculate according to sales positions and territorial assignments.

**(2) Stability of Income:** The remuneration plan should be such which could provide regular income to the sales force.

**(3) Based on Merits:** The remuneration plan should be based on individual merits, ability and efficiency of the salesman. It should have the magnetic power of attracting able and efficient salesman to the enterprise.

**(4) Guarantee of Fair wage:** A good remuneration plan for the salesman should give guarantee for a fair amount of remuneration which can satisfy the requirements of his family. A remuneration plan which does not give guarantee for a fair wage may create dissatisfaction and instability.

**(5) Attractive:** A good remuneration plan should be attractive and encouraging so as to get efficient persons and retain able, efficient and experienced sales-force.

**(6) Lower Administrative Cost:** The remuneration plan should bear the minimum administrative cost so that the same may be implemented by the enterprise.

**(7) Timely:** Any remuneration plan, however, adequate, attractive, fair and equitable may be it is bound to lose its weight if the payment to salesman in not made within the expected time. Money earned has value if it is received in the neck of the hour.

**(8) Incentive Oriented:** The remuneration plan should provide continuous incentive to the salesmen so as to evoke loyalty, sincerity and hard working on the part of a salesman. For instance, it should have provision the commission on sales besides the salary.

**(9) Flexible:** The remuneration plan should be flexible so that it may provide satisfaction to all types of salesmen working on different posts in different areas.

**(10) Economical:** The remuneration plan should be quite economical. It should not be a burden to the management as the purpose of sound remuneration plan is to increase the sales and profits at least cost. As per experts it should not go beyond 5 to 16 percent of the net sales value.

**(11) Fair to sales force :** The remuneration should be such in which the salesman might feel that he is paid sufficiently in relation to his qualifications, experience, ability, cost of living and his efforts etc. It must have provision for promotion.

**(12) Fair to Management:** The remuneration plan should also be fair to management, i.e. related to the volume of sales and be reasonable to the work turned out by the salesmen.

**(13) Competitive:** The remuneration plan should be competitive. It should develop the spirit of competition amongst the salesmen. The remuneration plan should provide superior income to superior performance.

**(14) Effective Control:** The remuneration plan should provide effective control of management on salesmen. According to Philip Kotler, "Management likes a plan which facilitates control over how salesmen spend their time. "It should be possible for the sales manager to bring to book a salesman who is not complying with the instructions and wasting away his efforts in non remunerative transactions.

**(15) Miscellaneous:** Besides the above, a sound remuneration plan should also be

(i) Helpful in increasing sales,

(ii) Personal

(iii) Evolve confidence of the salesmen,

(iv) Promptness in payments

(v) Developing active cooperation amongst the salesmen and finally

(vi) Able to raise the morale of the salesmen.

**MAIN OBJECTIVES OF A REMUNERATION PLAN FOR A SALESMAN.**

(*i*) The first and foremost objective of the remuneration plan is to keep work attractive and maintain top flight sales force.

(*ii*) Create incentives for salesman to work productively and efficiently.

(*iii*) Achieving maximum sales

(*iv*) Equip the management with power to direct and control the activities of the salesmen in achieving the goals of the business.

(*v*) Eliminate unsuitable and incompetent persons from he sales job.

(*vi*) Make the salesman feel highly of his job and security of his income.

(*vii*) Motivate the sales force to respond favourably to the customer's needs.

(*viii*) Evoke the loyalty, faithfulness, spirit of cooperation and sincerity amongst the salesmen.

(*ix*) Maintain an effective coordination between the efforts of the salesmen, results and remuneration paid to them.

(*x*) Economical i.e. achieving maximum sales at the minimum cost.

## METHODS OF REMUNERATING SALESMEN

The following methods are being used in connection with remuneration of salesmen:

1. Straight salary or fixed salary method
2. Straight commission on sales method
3. Combination of salary and commission method or salary plus commission method.
4. Salary plus share in profits method
5. Drawing account and commission method
6. Salary plus bonus method
7. Special task method

### (1) Straight Salary or Fixed Salary Method

It is the oldest, simplest, easiest and most common method of remunerating a salesman. Under this method a fixed amount every month is paid to the salesman irrespective of the volume of sales turned out by him. In this way there is no extra incentive to do hard work for increasing sales.

**Advantages :**

(1) This method provides maximum security and stability of earnings to the salesman. A total fixed monthly income is guaranteed to the salesman.

(2) It enables the salesman to give his full attention to selling for the risk involved in the time lost falls on the enterprise.

(3) This method provides management with power to control and direct salesman's efforts on most productive lines as they deem fit.

(4) It is the simplest and easiest method of remunerating the salesman. Straight salary is easy to compute and requires little accounting.

(5) It builds up a sales force which is loyal and contented.

(6) This method is suitable specially to new trainees/entrants.

(7) It is flexible and adjustable to the changing selling situations.

**Disadvantage or Limitations**

(1) This method does not provide any incentive to the sales force to work hard. The salesman merely becomes an order-taker.

(2) It is difficult to differentiate between incompetent and competent salesman.

(3) The salary fixed is unrelated to sales efforts and is merely a fixed cost of distribution

(4) This method lacks flexibility

(5) The initiative, skill, experience, efficiency and efforts of salesman bear no consideration at all

(6) This method might lead to discontentment and dissatisfaction particularly amongst the old salesmen

(7) Fixing remuneration is really very difficult as we cannot measure all salesmen with a common yard-stick like a piece of cloth. Individual differences warrant differences in salaries.

### (2) Straight Commission on Sales Method

Under this method only commission is paid to the salesman on the volume of sales. Thus a salesman who sells more gets more commission and the one who sells less gets less commission. In this way compensation of a salesman is based on his efforts measured in terms of volume and value of sales. The rate of commission may be progressive or regressive as sales volume increases or decreases.

**Advantages**

(1) This method provides maximum financial incentive to work hard as per his capacity

(2) This method is flexible

(3) It is both fair and economical

(4) Best salesmen are attracted to the sales organization

(5) The risks of bearing fixed selling expenses in the case of decline of sales are avoided

(6) The salesmen are motivated to increase sales to the maximum extent so as to get maximum commission

(7) Salesmen can use their selling time more efficiently and profitably

(8) High rate of commission may be offered for the sale of a product, provided the enterprise desires to emphasis economise.

(9) A direct relationship between sales and selling cost is established.

(10) Selling targets can be achieved quite easily.

**Disadvantages or Limitations**

(1) This method would cause unnecessary hardship to the salesmen when sales are on a decline though there is no fault of the salesmen, such as, where there is a depression in the market or the purchasing power of the money has gone down and people are not anxious to make purchases.

(2) The salesman is not sure of getting a living wage

(3) There are unscrupulous employers who have, by means of false promises, exploited preferably by new and inexperienced salesmen

(4) Customer's services suffer adversely

(5) Salesmen attach less importance to the new prospective customers. Their efforts are mostly confined to old customers only

(6) The salesmen may use high pressure tactics to increase the volume of sales in order to earn more commission. In this way the goodwill of the firm will get damaged in the long run

(7) This method gives incentive to make credit sales resulting in rapid increase of bad debts

(8) The control exercised by the sales manager over the salesman is weakened considerably.

### (3) Combination of Salary and Commission Method or Salary plus Commission Method

Under this method of remunerating salesman both salary and commission are paid to the salesman. In this way it is the combination of both the method i.e. straight salary and commission paid to the salesman. Besides normal monthly salary the salesmen are also paid a reasonable commission on sales in the form of incentive. This method removes the drawbacks of both the methods. That is why it is the most popular method of remunerating salesmen now-a-days.

**Advantages**

(1) Sales are increased considerably

(2) This method motivates the salesman to work hard so as to earn maximum commission besides usual regular salary.

(3) It provides safety and security to the salesmen in times of depression etc

(4) It provides satisfaction to the salesman and also increases his efficiency

(5) Best salesmen are attracted to the sales organization

(6) It provides incentive to both new and old salesmen

(7) Salesmen approach new and potential customers and thus new sales opportunities are developed.

(8) Under this method the salesman is not in a position to avoid unproductive lines of work, such as, writing of daily reports, and communication of market information etc. because he is paid monthly salary also

(9) It is easy to evaluate the salesman. The salesman who gets maximum commission is deemed to be a most competent and efficient salesman

(10) It is a flexible method of remunerating salesmen.

**Disadvantages or Limitations**

(1) It proves a burden on the enterprise during depression period

(2) The administrative cost of this method is quite high

(3) There is every possibility for a salesman to adopt high pressure tactics in selling so as to earn more commission which may in the long run affect adversely the goodwill of the firm and the relationship with the customers

(4) The enterprise suffers loss during the absence of the salesman as it is required to pay his salary during his absence also

(5) Determination and calculation of commission causes delay in payment of the commission. In this way, it causes anxiety and dissatisfaction to the salesman. Sometimes this tactic is used intentionally by the sales manager so that the salesman may not leave the job at least in the middle of the session

### (4) Salary plus a Share in Profits only

Under this method the salesman is given some percentage in the profits besides his regular monthly salary. The share is given in the overall profits of the enterprise. The most outstanding feature of this system is that the salesman participates in profits only and not in loss, if any.

**Advantages**

(1) Creates healthy relations between the firm and the salesmen

(2) Since the salesman is also a partner in the firm he makes every possible effort of increasing sales.

(3) The salesman performs his duties more honestly, sincerely, efficiently and economically and with full devotion.

(4) The morale of the salesman is raised considerably.

(5) Participation in profits is an incentive to hard labour and an additional source of income to the salesman

(6) The administrative cost in the management of this method is reduced

(7) There is rapid increase in profits of the enterprise.

**Disadvantages or Limitations**

(1) In case of loss, the entire burden falls on the firm

(2) Profit is awarded to all the salesmen equally whereas they differ in skill, ability, capacity and efficiency

(3) Profits of the enterprise fluctuate. With the result the income of the salesmen also fluctuates. Hence the standard of living is adversely affected

(4) The method is usually opposed by the owners of the enterprises where the profits are high.

### (5) Drawing Account and Commission Method

Under this method salesman is paid a fixed amount of money weekly/fortnightly/monthly and the same is transferred to his drawing account. After a definite period (half yearly or yearly as the case may be) the amount of drawings standing in his name is adjusted by the commission which they have earned on sales made by them. In case the commission exceeds the drawings, the balance is paid in cash to the salesman. On the contrary, if the drawings exceed to the commission, the balance remains standing in his account and it is carried forward to be adjusted later on.

**Advantages**

(1) It provides a regular assured amount of money to salesman to cover his living expenses

(2) This method is in the interest of the firm because the salesman makes every possible effort to earn by way of commission at least that amount of money so as to cover the drawings made during a given period. Thereby the sales are also increased

(3) It assures freedom to the salesman

(4) It is both fair and economical

(5) Good and efficient salesmen are attracted and incapable and inefficient salesmen are compelled to leave the job automatically

(6) The risks of bearing fixed selling expenses in the case of decline of sales are avoided

(7) A direct relation between sales and selling costs is established.

**Disadvantages or Limitations**

(1) Under this method it is difficult to exercise control on the activities of the salesman

(2) In case the drawings exceed the amount of commission, it becomes difficult to recover the overdrawn amount from the salesman. Under such circumstances a salesman usually leaves the job and runs away

(3) Salesmen are likely to use high pressure tactics to increase the sales volume and thus earn more commission. It is likely to damage the goodwill of the enterprise in the long run

(4) Customer's services are also adversely affected. Salesmen pay less importance to new prospective customers.

### (6) Salary plus Bonus Method

Under this method salesmen are given bonus besides the regular monthly salary. A bonus is nothing more than an extra commission paid on net sales after a predetermined value has been reached. For example, a salesman is required to sell products to the extent of Rs. 1,00,000 to earn his bonus. If a salesman has reached this predetermined value then only he is entitled to get bonus in addition to his salary. The idea behind the bonus method of remunerating the salesman is to provide incentive to increase the sales. Bonuses are also given for special achievements, such as, selling particular or special products, making new customers, making collections, cutting down selling expenses, increasing profits etc.

**Advantages**

(1) It develops the spirit of cooperation amongst the salesmen

(2) The total sales are increased

(3) It reduces the turnover of the sales department

(4) It provides motivation to salesman to increase his total income by increasing the sales of the enterprise

(5) Profits of the enterprise are increased

(6) Morale of the salesman is increased

(7) This method provides incentive to the salesman to do hard work and increase his efficiency.

**Disadvantages or Limitations**

(1) The administrative cost in the management of this method is increased

(2) The method of calculating the bonus is complex and is not easily understood even by an intelligent salesman. Thereby it may lead to misunderstanding between him and the sales manager

(3) The amount of bonus is likely to fluctuate every year, thereby causing adverse effect on the budget or the salesman. It might develop the overspending habit.

### (7) Special Task Method

Under this method the salesman is assigned a special task to perform and the remuneration is also settled accordingly. As soon as the task is completed, the salesman is remunerated at the prescribed rate. If the performance exceeds the task assigned to him, separate payment is made for additional performance. The special task may include collection of outstanding dues, selling specific items which require special skill, knowledge and tact; creating new customers; making sales in a new territory or market etc. it is a challenging salesmanship.

**Advantages**

(1) It is the best method of remunerating for special task performance

(2) The morale of the organization and that of salesman is increased

(3) It provides additional income to the experienced, competent, talented and risk-bearing salesman

(4) The goodwill as well as the sales of the enterprise is increased

(5) No regular and separate salesman is required to be appointed and thereby the enterprise is relived from any additional burden.

**Disadvantages or Limitations**

(1) This method of remunerating salesman is totally unsuitable for new salesmen

(2) It is difficult to evaluate the amount of remuneration to be paid to the salesman

(3) The routine sales are likely to be disturbed.

## BEST METHOD OF REMUNERATING SALESMEN

Best remuneration method is that which provides maximum satisfaction to all concerned i.e. enterprise, salesman and also the customer. After studying the advantages and disadvantages of all the methods, we conclude that 'combination of salary and commission method' is the best and adequate method to secure good business. Besides providing a fixed and regular income to the salesman the method motivates him to increase sales to the maximum so as to increase his commission. On the contrary, the enterprise is also benefited in the sense that increase in sales leads to increase in profits and thereby overall development and progress of the enterprise. Further, the customers too are provided better services and thus it leads to good and everlasting relationship with the new and old customers. That is why this method is most popular among salesmen and the firms.

### Factors determining remuneration to sales-force

The remuneration/compensation plans for different organizations vary from organization to organization. However, there are some common factors as given below, which may influence the remuneration structure of sales force :

(1) Ability of the organization to pay

(2) Existence of nature of competition in the market

(3) Size of the market

(4) Nature of product i.e. consumer or industrial

(5) Whether the product and market, both are new or old

(6) Government laws and regulations

(7) Emphasis on advertisement

(8) Salary / Compensation paid by other organizations in the same fields.

(9) Price of the product i.e. low or high

(10) Incentives payable to salesman

(11) Required ability of the salesman. For example, the more educated, trained, possessing technical qualifications and experienced salesman will demand higher remuneration than that with less qualified, trained and experienced.

(12) Reputation and goodwill of the organization.

## REVIEW QUESTIONS

1. What is a good remuneration Plan?
2. What is straight (or) fixed salary method?
3. What is Salary plus commission method?
4. What is salary plus bonus method?
5. What are the characteristics of an ideal/good remuneration plan?
6. State the common factors that influence the remuneration structure of a salesman.
7. State the merits of a good remuneration plan for a salesman
8. What are various methods is remunerating a salesman
9. Which is the best method for remurating Salesman - Why?

# 13 Motivating Sales-Force

## MEANING OF MOTIVATION

Motivation is a psychological set of forces influencing the behaviour of an individual. It involves a complex combination of individual needs, desires, discomforts, aspirations, emotions and expectations. Motivation is the ability to influence sales-force in such a way as to get them to do what you expect them to do. To motivate a sales-force, a sales manager is expected to know the needs, emotions, aspirations and expectations of his salesmen, their emotional, mental and physical needs, why they work? What they want to get for their work? What are their attitudes towards the company, their work and superiors? According to experts, 75% of the sales are turned out by just 25% of the salesmen. It is the motivation, which makes the sales-force to intensify its desire and willingness to use its potential effectively or the achievement of sales organizational objectives, goals and targets.

## DEFINITIONS OF MOTIVATION:

Motivation is a difficult concept. Different authors have defined motivation in various ways. The main definitions of motivation are given below:

(1) *Sharetle* defines "Motivation as a reported urge of tension to move in a given direction to achieve a certain goal".

(2) According to *Dalton E. Mcfarland*, "Motivation refers to the way in which urges, desires, aspirations, and strivings or needs direct, control or explain the behaviour of human beings."

(3) According to *W.G.Scott*, "Motivation means a process of stimulating people to action to accomplish desired goals."

(4) According to *Michael J.Jucious*, "Motivation is the act of stimulating some one or oneself to get a desired course of action or to push the right button to get a desired reaction".

From the above definition we can conclude that, "Motivation is linked with work. It is a process of inducing, inspiring and energizing the salesman to work willingly, with zeal, initiative, confidence, satisfaction and in an integrated manner to work at one's highest pitch to achieve desired goals and targets." Motivation is a morale boosting activity.

## FORCES OF MOTIVATION

Before motivating the sales-force, the sales manager should have a thorough understanding of the motives, impulses or urges behind the work. He should create a proper environment, climate and tempo, and should identify the forces that motivate salesmen to gear up productive effort. The forces or prerequisites of motivation are as follows:

(1) **Proper Environment**: It is the working environment that influences the attitude of the salesman towards his work and performance. The most important aspect of environment is how the sales-force looks at it, and not how sales management views it. The salesman expects a proper working environment which should not only satisfy his needs but also encourage him to work more sincerely and efficiently.

(2) **Tempo**: Tempo also plays an important role in boosting morale of the sales-force. It has an important bearing on selling process. A good working tempo attracts and motivates the sales-force to work with due speed, identify opportunities, solve problems, take necessary decisions and implement them accordingly. For instance, Tata's sales department has a good tempo of working and achieving desired goals. Even salesman working at the lowest cadre feels pride that he is working in Tata's Group.

(3) **Fair Pay Packet (Remuneration):** It is a dominant motive because every salesman working in an organization expects a decent living for himself and his dependants. The pay packet given to a salesman should not only satisfy his needs but also be comparable with his colleagues in his own organization and competitive organizations with equal performance and responsibilities. Hence the pay packet (remuneration) provided to sales-force should not only be fair but also attractive and assured one.

(4) **Recognition and Praise: Salesmen**, like any other human being, seek recognition and praise for their achievements in the field of sales. Failure to compliment and praise on the part of sales management is ignoring a vital need in salesman's nature and having deeper impact on sales performance.

(5) **Job security;** Job security is also an important prerequisite. Every Salesman, like other workers, expects that his job is fully secured and he will continue to retain his job so long his work and performance is quite satisfactory. However, it is unfortunate that salesman's job in India is most unsafe as he can be turned out on any day on one excuse or the other. It is evident too from the newspapers. In most of the Indian business enterprises, salesman's job is considered as a seasonal job. It is true especially in book publishing and selling business. Hence job security to salesman is the need of the hour for his own development and also for the future development of the business enterprise in which he is employed. Job security does not mean that the salesman should be made permanent from the date of appointment. It only means protection from arbitrary discharge or dismissal or transfer.

(6) **Opportunity for progress and Advancement:** Salesman's job like any other job, should have ample opportunities for progress and advancement. Any business enterprise that fails to provide such an opportunity for progress and advancement will be responsible for high sales force turnover by depriving the basic needs and creating dissatisfaction, corruption and frustration among the salesmen.

(7) **Targets and Goal Oriented**: Motivation to salesmen should be target and goal oriented. It will serve as an important measuring rod of work, performance and achievement of the salesman. It is in the interest of both the salesmen and the sales management.

(8) **Honest and Competent Leadership:** If leadership from sales manager down to sales supervisors is honest, competent, sympathetic and capable of understanding sales-force's hopes and aspirations, emotions and sentiments, prospects and problems, motives and attitudes, they will be able to win their confidence, cooperation and loyalty. The leadership should be competent to lead, excel, control, maintain discipline and motivate their salesmen.

(9) **Job Satisfaction:** The sales management should place sales force properly according to their qualifications, merits, experience, aptitudes, interests and capacities. The well-placed salesmen take pride, interest and initiative in their work and performance and derive job satisfaction. Job satisfaction leads to security and realization of goals.

(10) **Opportunity for self-expression**: Salesmen have their own views, attitudes, ideas, suggestions etc., which they want to express, assert their personalities and exploit their latest talents and abilities.

(11) **Pride in Selling:** Besides Job security and job satisfaction the salesmen should feel pride in selling as a vocation. There was a time when selling was looked upon as degrading and disgraceful. But now it is not so. It has been developed as a full-fledged profession. The significance of selling must be emphasized in preparing salesmen. They should be given an understanding that they are doing creative, socially acceptable and respected job.

(12) **Other Motivations:** Besides the above, several other physical and psychological motivations may be offered by the sales management to tone up sales-force morale and motivate them towards achieving stated objectives and targets.

## OBJECTIVES OF SALESMAN AND MOTIVATION

The sole objective of salesmen motivation is to generate within a salesman the will to work with a view to achieving results and surpassing stated targets and goals. This objective is achieved by linking the success of the project to the interest of the individual. The easiest example is salesman's commission. Salesmen have to increase their commission earnings and through their efforts the company achieves its budget. According the Prof. Johnson, "The main objective of motivation is to encourage salesmen for improving their efficiently so as to achieve their goals." The objectives of motivation, in general, are as follows:

1. To encourage salesmen to maximize sales
2. To encourage for increasing their efficiency
3. To raise the morale of the sales-force
4. To achieve the active and full support of the sales-force
5. To develop sound and cordial mutual relations amongst the salesmen.
6. To establish good and sound relations between the salesmen and sales management.
7. To satisfy the economic, social and mental needs of the salesmen.
8. To provide job satisfaction to salesmen.
9. To encourage salesmen to improve the quality of their working or service
10. To provide job security, fair pay packet and good working conditions to sales force.

## NEED, SIGNIFICANCE OR IMPORTANCE OF MOTIVATION TO SALESMEN

It has been demonstrated conclusively by the researches conducted in the field of motivation that motivation has a direct bearing on the salesmen. Increase in motivation leads to better performance and decrease in motivation leads to poorer performance. In the word of Allen, "Poorly motivated people can nullify the soundest organization". The success of any sales organization depends on the efficiency and method of working of its sales force. The sales organization can appoint efficient and able salesmen, compel them to be physically and mentally present on the job but it is not essential to have their devotion, loyalty, sincerity, initiative, zeal, cooperation, interest and confidence. These can be achieved only by motivation. Motivation is linked with will to work. It is the act of changing the psychology of a salesman to make him to work better. It is the task of intensifying the desire to work at one's highest pitch, It is to encourage, stimulate, elevate, to lift up productivity. In short, the need, significance or importance of motivation is evident from the following:

1. Motivation encourages the sales-force to work with utmost efficiency.
2. Motivation is a goal-oriented process. It directs the salesmen to achieve the desired goals and targets within the prescribed time.
3. Motivation develops cooperation amongst the salesmen as well as in between the salesmen and the sales management.
4. Motivation is a morale boosting activity. It raises the morale of the sales force which is in the interest of the business enterprise too.
5. Motivation increases the working capacity of the sales force.
6. Motivation plays a crucial role in developing human relations.
7. Motivation develops interest and devotion of the sales force towards their work.
8. Motivation is a must for satisfying the economic, social and psychological needs of the salesmen.
9. Motivation provides job satisfaction to the salesmen.
10. Motivation creates a sense of responsibility, loyalty, interest, confidence and enthusiasm among the salesmen.

In short, motivation ensures high-level performance, effective utilization of resources, high morale, cordial human relations, sense of responsibility, zeal, initiative, unity of purpose, confidence, satisfaction, mutual trust and respect loyalty, discipline, easy acceptance of organizational changes, low salesmen turnover, absenteeism and labour unrest.

## METHODS OF MOTIVATION:

Methods of Motivation may be classified under the following two major heads:

I. Individual and Group Basis Motivation.

II. Financial and Non financial Motivation

**Individual Basis Motivation:** Individual basis motivation is that motivation which is provided to every salesman individually in accordance with the nature of his job as entrusted to him by the sales manager/management. Individual motivation is most effective in stimulating the interest of salesmen. It may be in the form of (i) personal meeting and conference between the salesmen and the sales manager, and (ii) personal correspondence between the salesmen and the sales manager/sales management.

**Group Basis Motivation:** Under this method of motivation, salesmen are motivated in groups or batches through conferences and conventions, organizing sales contests, publications, booklets and handbooks, motion pictures, participating programmes, suggestion systems and group compensation plans etc.

## REVIEW QUESTIONS

1. What do you mean by motivation?
2. What are various methods of motivation?
3. What are the various prerequisites forces of motivation
4. Explain the significance of motivation to salesmen

# 14 Sales Incentives

## MEANING OF SALES INCENTIVES

Incentive means that which incites or has a tendency to incite action. A sales incentive can be defined as anything that incities the salesman's action. Sales incentives induce the salesman to work to his full capacity or in some cases higher than that. Sales incentives influence the 'will to work' of the sales force so as to achieve the desired goal. It is the function of the sales management to provide incentives to the salesmen which induces them to increase sales at minimum costs. It also raises the morale of the sales force.

## DIFFERENCE BETWEEN INCENTIVE AND MOTIVATION

Often people are confused about the meaning of incentive and motivation. Incentive is something which incites or tends to incite towards some determination. Thus incentive is an external stimulus that activates need. On the other hand, motivation refers to an activated need, an active desire or wish. Thus, conceptual difference between motivation and incentive is that incentive is the means to motivation.

## METHODS OF PROVIDING INCENTIVES TO SALESMEN

The companies for providing incentives to the salesmen use different methods. They may be classified under the following two major heads:

(*i*) Financial Incentives

(*ii*) Non financial incentives

1. **Financial Incentives:** Financial Incentives induce the sales force to work hard by offering them reward for better performance in terms of money. The normal trend is to pay more attention to financial incentives to the sales personnel. Financial incentives may be given in two forms. It may be in the form of direct monetary payments, like much adequate salaries and wages, commission on sales, bonus for additional sales, expense allowance etc. Financial incentives may also be in the form of indirect monetary rewards, commonly known as fringe benefits. This consists of pension, provident fund schemes, health insurance, paid vacations etc;
2. **Non financial Incentives**: It is not always correct that money alone provides incentive. We must remember that money is a means and not an end in itself. Non financial incentives include all other influences, planned or unplanned, which stimulate the salesman to work hard. Non financial incentives play a significant role in raising the morale of the sales force to do greater and better work. Non-financial incentives include sales conventions and meetings, sales contests, bulletins and handbooks, sales quotas, honours and rewards,

recognition, emotional security, fair and sympathetic treatment, authority and responsibility, participation in management, promotion, effective personel relations, personal letters, training programmes, freedom to express himself etc.

## SALESMANSHIP AND PSYCHOLOGY

Psychology plays a crucial role in selling. The sale is effected only if prospect is convinced in his own mind that it will be beneficial for him to make purchases of a particular product. In this act of purchase the prospect's mind goes through a number of mental stages. The number and the type of mental stages vary from prospect to prospect. For example, some of the mental stages through which the prospect's mind normally passes would be:

(*i*) Attention
(*ii*) Interest aroused
(*iii*) Knowledge increased
(*iv*) Adjustment to requirements
(*v*) Consideration of the suitability of the product concerned
(*vi*) Desire to possess the product concerned
(*vii*) Consideration of the price
(*viii*) Reaction point, and
(*ix*) Satisfaction.

Among the above, the reaction is the most important. The reaction point is the psychological point, i.e. the point at which the prospect makes his final decision. The reaction point is deemed to be positive or favourable if the prospect decides to purchase the product concerned. ON the contrary, the reaction point is deemed to be negative or unfavourable if the prospect decides not to purchase the product concerned. Hence, sincere effort should be made towards this point and its significance should be clearly and fully understood. If the reaction point is positive then the final action would be the purchase of the product so offered. The product must be presented in such a manner as to make the most favourable impression on the prospect that the product is profitable, useful and acceptable to the prospect. This requires considerable skill or art on the part of the salesman.

In short, the study of psychology assists the salesman in the following ways:

(1) **In welcoming the prospect:** When a prospect enters the shop/business house he expects a warm welcome from the salesman. Only the study of psychology can tell the salesman as to the type of welcome, which a prospect expects from him. This provides the initial satisfaction to the prospect.

(2) **In finding out the Level, Taste and Need of the Prospect:** On the basis of the study of psychology, the salesman can find out the level, taste and need of the prospect. Interest is aroused by showing the product according to his level, taste and need.

(3) **In studying the Buying Motives of the Prospect:** A prospect has different buying motives for purchasing a product. Hence it is essential that the salesman should know the buying motives of the prospect. However, it is possible only through the study of psychology. The work of the salesman becomes easier if he acquires the basic knowledge of the buying motives of the prospect.

(4) **In finding out the Desires and Tastes of the Prospect:** Actually speaking, salesmanship is the technique of arousing interest of the prospect, finding out his tastes and thereby converting them into need. This is also possible through the study of psychology. The desire and the taste can be developed through a proper sales presentation and sales talk. For example, if the salesman is selling cosmetics of a popular manufacturer, he should demonstrate it to the prospect by showing how fine the quality appears. The prospect should be asked to smell the sweet fragrance of the perfume used. The interest thus arose is automatically converted into desire by convincing him of the benefits, which he will get through the use of the cosmetics.

(5) **In finding out the Mental Position of the Prospect:** The study of psychology assists the salesman in finding out the mental position of the prospect. The salesman should convince that this particular product once will satisfy his need by making a sincere effort. IN order to convince the prospect, the objections raised by him should be met adequately. Once he is convinced, he would be ready to purchase the product.

From the above discussion, it is clear that the study of psychology is a must for salesmanship and both of them are closely related.

## "SALESMEN ARE BORN, NOT MADE."

Old style managers are of the opinion that salesmen are born and not made. They argue that an inborn salesman has inherent qualities suitable for the job. Suitable business conditions are provided to him in his family since birth and thus he is adapted to the prevailing business conditions. His personality is also developed in and around his family. Most of his habits such as intelligence, knowledge, good physique, pica sing manners, knowledge of the power of product understanding, power of understanding the psychology of the customer and personality are factors depending on his inborn qualities and features. In this way if the father is a good salesman then his son will also be a good salesman. He acquires the qualities of a good salesman from his father.

On the contrary, modern managers are of the opinion that salesman are made and not born. The extensive activities that are carried on by salesman need talents enough to become sales people. Personality and family background alone cannot make an individual a successful salesman. Whatever inherent qualities a born salesman may possess this does not mean that he can get on well without training. Only a good training programme will equip him with abilities needed for a good salesman. Evidently a good salesman is made. There is nothing as born salesman. The personal traits combined with good training makes the person a good salesman. Salesmen are recruited, motivated, trained, compensated, supervised and controlled so as to fulfill the difficult and challenging task of selling.

From the above discussions it is evident that a good salesman is made and not born. However, if he possesses inborn qualities then his task becomes easier, successful and challenging.

## REVIEW QUESTIONS

1. What do you mean by an incentive?
2. Name the methods of providing incentives to salesman
3. How the study of psychology helps a salesman ?
4. "Sales men are born and not made" – Discuss.

# 15 Sales Promotion

In a time when customers are exposed daily to a nearly infinite amount of promotional messages, many marketers are discovering that advertising alone is not enough to move members of a target market to take action, such as getting them to try a new product. Instead, marketers have learned that to meet their goals they must use additional promotional methods in conjunction with advertising.

Other marketers have found that certain characteristics of their target market (e.g., small but geographically dispersed) or characteristics of their product (e.g., highly complex) make advertising a less attractive option. For these marketers better results may be obtained using other promotional approaches and may lead to directing all their promotional spending to non-advertising promotions.

Finally, the high cost of advertising may drive many to seek alternative, lower cost promotional techniques to meet their promotion goals.

In Part 15 of our detailed Principles of Marketing Tutorial we continue our discussion of promotion decisions by looking at a second promotion mix item: sales promotion. Sales promotions are used widely in many industries and especially by marketers selling to consumers. We will see that the objectives of sales promotion are quite different than advertising and are specifically designed to encourage customer response.

## WHAT IS SALES PROMOTION?

Sales promotion describes promotional methods using special short-term techniques to persuade members of a target market to respond or undertake certain activity. As a reward, marketers offer something of value to those responding generally in the form of lower cost of ownership for a purchased product (e.g., lower purchase price, money back) or the inclusion of additional value-added material (e.g., something more for the same price).

Sales promotions are often confused with advertising. For instance, a television advertisement mentioning a contest awarding winners with a free trip to a Caribbean Island may give the contest the appearance of advertising. While the delivery of the marketer's message through television media is certainly labeled as advertising, What is contained in the message, namely the contest, is considered a sales promotion. The factors that distinguish between the two promotional approaches are:

(*i*) Whether the promotion involves a short-term value proposition (e.g., the contest is only offered for a limited period of time), and

(*ii*) The customer must perform some activity in order to be eligible to receive the value proposition (e.g., customer must enter contest).

The inclusion of a timing constraint and an activity requirement are hallmarks of sales promotion.

Sales promotions are used by a wide range of organizations in both the consumer and business markets, though the frequency and spending levels are much greater for consumer product marketers. One estimate by the Promotion Marketing Association suggests that in US alone spending on sales promotion exceeds that of advertising.

## OBJECTIVES OF SALES PROMOTION

Sales promotion is a tool used to achieve most of the five major promotional objectives discussed in Part 12: Promotion Decisions:

- Building Product Awareness – Several sales promotion techniques are highly effective in exposing customers to products for the first time and can serve as key promotional components in the early stages of new product introduction. Additionally, as part of the effort to build product awareness, several sales promotion techniques possess the added advantage of capturing customer information at the time of exposure to the promotion. In this way sales promotion can act as an effective customer information gathering tool (i.e., sales lead generation), which can then be used as part of follow-up marketing efforts.
- Creating Interest – Marketers find that sales promotions are very effective in creating interest in a product. In fact, creating interest is often considered the most important use of sales promotion. In the retail industry an appealing sales promotions can significantly increase customer traffic to retail outlets. Internet marketers can use similar approaches to bolster the number of website visitors. Another important way to create interest is to move customers to experience a product. Several sales promotion techniques offer the opportunity for customers to try products for free or at low cost.
- Providing Information – Generally sales promotion techniques are designed to move customers to some action and are rarely simply informational in nature. However, some sales promotions do offer customers access to product information. For instance, a promotion may allow customers to try a fee-based online service free for several days. This free access may include receiving product information via email.
- Stimulating Demand – Next to building initial product awareness, the most important use of sales promotion is to build demand by convincing customers to make a purchase. Special promotions, especially those that lower the cost of ownership to the customer (e.g., price reduction), can be employed to stimulate sales.
- Reinforcing the Brand – Once customers have made a purchase sales promotion can be used to both encourage additional purchasing and also as a reward for purchase loyalty (see loyalty programs below). Many companies, including airlines and retail stores, reward good or "preferred" customers with special promotions, such as email "special deals" and surprise price reductions at the cash register.

## TYPES OF SALES PROMOTION

Sales promotion can be classified based on the primary target audience to whom the promotion is directed. These include :

- Consumer Market Directed - Possibly the most well-known methods of sales promotion are those intended to appeal to the final consumer. Consumers are exposed to sales promotions nearly everyday, and as discussed later, many buyers are conditioned to look for sales promotions prior to making purchase decisions.
- Trade Market Directed – Marketers use sales promotions to target all customers including partners within their channel of distribution. Trade promotions are initially used to entice channel members to carry marketer's products and, once products are stocked, marketers utilize promotions to strengthen the channel relationship.
- Business-to-Business Market Directed – A small, but important, sub-set of sales promotions are targeted to the business-to-business market. While these promotions may not carry the glamour associated with consumer or trade promotions, B-to-B promotions are used in many industries.

## CONSUMER SALES PROMOTION

Consumer sales promotions encompass a variety of short-term promotional techniques designed to induce customers to respond in some way. The most popular consumer sales promotions are directly associated with product purchasing. These promotions are intended to enhance the value of a product purchased by either reducing the overall cost of the product (i.e., get same product but for less money) or by adding more benefit to the regular purchase price (i.e., get more for the money).

While trying a promotion to an immediate purchase is a major use of consumer sales promotion, it is not the only one. As we noted above, promotion techniques can be used to achieve other objectives such as building brand loyalty or creating product awareness. Consequently, a marketer's promotional toolbox contains a large variety of consumer promotions.

1. Coupons
2. Rebates
3. Promotional Pricing
4. Trade-In
5. Loyalty Programes
6. Sampling and Free Trials
7. Free Product
8. Premiums
9. Contests and Sweepstakes
10. Demonstrations
11. Personal Appearances

## COUPONS

Most consumers are quite familiar with this form of sales promotion, which offers purchasers price savings or other incentives when the coupon is redeemed at the time of purchase. Coupons are short-term in nature since most (but not all) carry an expiration date after which the value may not be received. Also, coupons require consumer involvement in order for value to be realized. In most cases involvement consists of the consumer making an effort to obtain the coupon (e.g., clip from newspaper) and then presenting it at the time of purchase.

Coupons are used widely by marketers across many retail industries and reach consumers in a number of different delivery formats including:

- Free-Standing Inserts (FSI) – Here coupon placement occurs loosely (i.e., inserted) within media, such as newspapers and direct mail, and may or may not require the customer to cut away from other material in order to use.
- Cross-Product – These consist of coupons placed within or on other products. Often a marketer will use this method to promote one product by placing the coupon inside another major selling product. For example, a pharmaceutical company may imprint a coupon for a cough remedy on the basis of a pain medication. Also, this delivery approach is used when two marketers have struck a cross promotion arrangement where each agree to undertake certain marketing activity for the other.
- Printout – A delivery method that is common in many food stores is to present coupons to a customer at the conclusion of the purchasing process. These coupons, which are often printed on the spot, are intended to be used for a future purchase and not for the current purchase which triggered the printing.
- Product Display – Some coupons are nearly impossible for customers to miss as they are located in close proximity to the product. In some instances coupons may be contained within a coupon dispenser fastened to the shelf holding the product while in other cases coupons may be attached to a special display (see POP display below) where customers can remove them (e.g., tear off).
- Internet – Several specialized websites, such as Hot Coupons.com, and even some manufacturer's sites, allow customers to print out coupons. These coupons are often the same ones appearing in other media, such as newspapers or direct mail. In other cases, coupons may be sent via email, though to be effective the customer's email program must be able to receive HTML email (and not text only) in order to maintain required design elements (e.g., bar code).
- Electronic – The Internet is also seeing the emergence of new non-printable coupons redeemable through website purchases. These electronic coupons are redeemed when the customer enters a designated coupon code during the purchase process

Rebates, like coupons, offer value to purchasers typically by lowering the customer's final cost for acquiring the product. While rebates share some similarities with coupons, they differ in several key aspects. First, rebates are generally handed or offered (e.g., accessible on the Internet) to customers after a purchase is made and cannot be used to obtain immediate savings in the way coupons are used. (So called "instant rebates", where customers receive price reductions at the time of purchase, have elements of both coupons and rebates, but for our purpose we will classify these as coupons due to the timing of the reward to the customer.)

Second, rebates often are request to the purchaser to submit personal data in order to obtain the rebate. For instance, customer identification, including name, address and contact information, is generally required to obtain a rebate. Also, the marketer may ask those seeking a rebate to provide additional data such as indicating the reason for making the purchase.

Third, unlike coupons that always offer value when used in a purchase (assuming it is accepted by the retailer), receiving a rebate only guarantees value if the customer takes actions. Marketers know that not all customers will respond to a rebate. Some will misplace or forget to submit the rebate while others may submit after a required deadline. Marketers factor in the non-redemption rate as they attempt to calculate the cost of the rebate promotion.

Finally, rebates tend to be used as a value enhancement in higher priced products compared to coupons. For instance, rebates are a popular promotion for automobiles and computer software where large amount of money may be returned to the customer.

## PROMOTIONAL PRICING

One of the most powerful sales promotion techniques is the short-term price reduction or, as known in some areas, "on sale" pricing. Lowering a product's selling price can have an immediate impact on demand, though marketers must exercise caution since the frequent use of this technique can lead customers to anticipate the reduction and, consequently, withhold purchase until the price reduction occurs again.

As we will see in a later tutorial, promotional pricing is also considered within the framework of the Price marketing mix component. More of this technique will be provided in that discussion.

## TRADE-IN

Trade-in promotions allow consumers to obtain lower prices by exchanging something the customer possess, such as an older product that the new purchase will replace. While the idea of gaining price breaks for trading in another product is most frequently seen with automobile sales, such promotions are used in other industries, such as computers and golf equipment, where the customer's exchanged product can be resold by the marketer in order to extract value.

## LOYALTY PROGRAMMES

Promotions that offer customers a reward, such as price discounts and free products, for frequent purchasing or other activity are called loyalty programmes. These promotions have been around for many years but grew rapidly in popularity when introduced in the airline industry as part of frequent-filer programmes. Loyalty programmes are also found in numerous other industries, including grocery, pizza purchasing and online book purchases, where they may also be known as club card programmes since members often must use a verification card as evidence of enrolment in the program.

Many loyalty programmes have become ingrained as part of the value offered by a marketer. That is, a retailer or marketing organization may offer loyalty programmes as general business practice. Under this condition loyalty programme does not qualify as a sales promotion since it does not fit the requirement of offering a short-term value (i.e., it is always offered). However, within a general business practice loyalty programme a sales promotion can be offered, such as special short-term offer that lowers the number of points needed to acquire a free product.

## SAMPLING AND FREE TRIALS

Enticing members of a target market to try a product is often easy when the trial comes at little or no cost to the customer. The use of samples and free trials may be the oldest of all sales promotion techniques dating back to when society advanced from a culture of self-subsistence to a culture of trade.

Sampling and free trials give customers the opportunity to experience products, often in small quantities or for a short duration, without purchasing the product. Today, these methods are used in almost all industries and are especially useful for getting customers to try a product for the first time.

## FREE PRODUCT

Some promotional methods offer free products but with the condition that a purchase be made. The free product may be in the form of additional quantities of the same purchased product (e.g., buy one, get one free) or specialty packages (e.g., value pack) that offer more quantity for the same price as regular packaging.

## PREMIUMS

Another form of sales promotion involving free merchandise is premium or "give-away" items. Premiums differ from samples and free product in that these often do not consist of the actual product, though there is often some connection. For example, a cellphone manufacturer may offer access to free downloadable ringtones for those purchasing a cellphone.

## CONTESTS AND SWEEPSTAKES

Consumers are often attracted to promotions where the potential value obtained is very high. In these promotions only a few lucky consumers receive the value offered in the promotion. Two types of promotions that offer high value are contests and sweepstakes.

Contests are special promotions awarding value to winners based on skills they demonstrate compared to others. For instance, a baking company may offer free vacations to winners of a baking contest. Contest award winners are often determined by a panel of judges.

Sweepstakes or drawings are not skill based but rather based on luck. Winners are determined by random selection. In some cases the chances of winning may be higher for those who make a purchase if entry into the sweepstake occurs automatically when a purchase is made. But in most cases, anyone is free to enter without the requirement to make a purchase.

A sub-set of both contests and sweepstakes are games, which come in a variety of formats such as scratch-off cards and collection of game pieces. Unlike contests and sweepstakes, which may not require purchase, to participate in a game customers may be required to make a purchase. In United States and other countries, where eligibility is based on purchase, games may be subjected to rigid legal controls and may actually fall under that category of lotteries, which are tightly controlled.

## DEMONSTRATIONS

Many products benefit from customers being shown how products are used through a demonstration. Whether the demonstration is experienced in-person or via video form, such as over the Internet, this promotional technique can produce highly effective results. Unfortunately, demonstrations are very expensive to produce. Costs involved in demonstrations include paying for the expense of the demonstrator, which can be high if the demonstrator is well-known (e.g., nationally known chef), and also paying for the space where the demonstration is given.

## PERSONAL APPEARANCES

An in-person appearance by someone of interest to the target market, such as an author, sports figure or celebrity, is another form of sales promotion capable of generating customer traffic to a physical location. However, as with demonstrations, personal appearance promotion can be expensive since the marketer normally must pay a fee for the person to appear.

## TRADE SALES PROMOTIONS

As noted in Part 12: Promotion Decisions, certain promotions can help "push" a product through the channel by encouraging channel members to purchase and also promote the product to their customers. For instance, a trade promotion aimed at retailers may encourage retailers to instruct their employees to promote a marketer's brand over competitors' offerings. With thousands of products competing for limited shelf space, spending on trade promotion is nearly equal to that spent on consumer promotions.

Many sales promotions aimed at building relationships with channel partners follow similar designs as those directed to consumers including promotional pricing, contests and free product. In addition to these, several other promotional approaches are specifically designed to appeal to trade partners. These approaches include:

1. Point-of-Purchase Displays
2. Advertising Support Programmes
3. Short Term Allowances
4. Sales Incentives or Push Money
5. Promotional Products
6. Trade Shows

## POINT-OF-PURCHASE DISPLAYS

Point of purchase (POP) displays are specially designed materials intended for placement in retail stores. These displays allow products to be prominently presented, often in high traffic areas, and thereby increase the probability the product will standout. POP displays come in many styles, though the most popular are ones allowing a product to stand alone, such as in the middle of a store aisle or sit at the end of an aisle (i.e., end-cap) where it will be exposed to heavy customer traffic.

For channel partners, POP displays can result in significant sales increases compared to sales levels in a normal shelf position. Also, many marketers will lower the per-unit cost of products in the POP display as an incentive for retailers to agree to include the display in their stores.

## ADVERTISING SUPPORT PROGRAMMES

In addition to offering promotional support in the form of physical displays, marketers can attract channel members' interest by offering financial assistance in the form of advertising money. These funds are often directed to retailers who then include the company's products in their advertising. In certain cases the marketer will offer to pay the entire cost of advertising, but more often, the marketer offers partial support known as co-op advertising funds.

## SHORT TERM TRADE ALLOWANCES

This promotion offers channel partners price breaks for agreeing to stock the product. In most cases the allowance is not only given as encouragement to purchase the product but also as an inducement to promote the product in other ways such as by offering attractive shelf space or store location, highlighting the product in company-produced advertising or website display, or by agreeing to have the retailer's sales personnel "talk-up" the product to customers.

Allowances can be in the form of price reductions (e.g. off-invoice promotion) and buy-back guarantees if the product does not sell in certain period of time.

### SALES INCENTIVES OR PUSH MONEY

Since sales promotions are intended to stimulate activity that leads to meeting promotional objectives, it makes sense that these can also apply to those in the organization who also affect sales. Thus, sales promotions are common place among an organization's sales force and customer service staff where they are used as incentives to help sell more of the marketer's product. Sometimes called push money, these promotions typically offer employees cash or prizes, such as trips, for those that meet sales requirements.

### PROMOTIONAL PRODUCTS

Among the most widely used methods of sales promotions is the promotional product; products labelled with the brand or company name that serve as reminders of the actual product. For instance, companies often hand out free calendars, coffee cups and pens that contain the product logo.

### TRADE SHOWS

One final type of trade promotion is the industry trade show (e.g. exhibitions, conventions). Trade shows are organized events that bring both industry buyers and sellers together in one central location. Spending on trade shows is one of the highest of all sales promotions. In fact, the Promotion Marketing Association estimates that, over (US) $20 billion is spent annually by marketers to participate in trade shows.

Marketers are attracted to trade shows since these offer the opportunity to reach a large number of potential buyers in one convenient setting. At these events most sellers attempt to capture the attention of buyers by setting up a display area to present their product offerings and meet with potential customers. These displays can range from a single table covering a small area to erecting specially built display booths that dominate the trade show floor.

### BUSINESS-TO-BUSINESS SALES PROMOTIONS

The use of sales promotion is not limited to consumer products marketing. In business-to-business markets sales promotions are also used as a means of moving customers to action. However, the promotional choices available to the B-to-B marketer are not as extensive as those found in the consumer or trade markets. For example, most B-to-B marketers do not use coupons as a vehicle for sales promotion with the exception of companies that sell to both consumer and business customers (e.g., products sold through office supply retailers). Rather, the techniques more likely to be utilized include:

1. price-reductions
2. free product
3. trade-in promotion
4. promotional products
5. trade shows

Of the promotions listed, trade shows are by far the mostly widely used sales promotion for B-to-B marketers.

## TRENDS IN SALES PROMOTION

Marketers who employ sales promotion as a key component in their promotional strategy should be aware of how the climate for these types of promotions is changing. The important trends in sales promotion include:

### CUSTOMERS' EXPECTATIONS

The onslaught of sales promotion activity over the last several decades has eroded the value of the short-term requirement to act on sales promotions. Many customers are conditioned to expect a promotion at the time of purchase otherwise they may withhold or even alter their purchase if a promotion is not present. For instance, food shoppers are inundated on a weekly basis with such a wide variety of sales promotions that their loyalty to certain products has been replaced by their loyalty to current value items (i.e., products with a sales promotion). For marketers, the challenge is to balance the advantages short-term promotions offer versus the potential to erode loyalty to the product.

### ELECTRONIC DELIVERY

Sales promotions are delivered to customers in many ways such as by mail, in-person or within print media. However, the Internet and mobile technologies, such as cellphones, present marketers with a number of new delivery options. For examples, the combination of mobile devices and geographic positioning technology will soon permit marketers to target promotions to a customer's physical location. This will allow retailers and other businesses to issue sales promotions, such as electronic coupons, to a customer's mobile device when they are near the location where the coupon can be used

### TRACKING

As we discussed in our coverage of advertising, tracking customer's response to marketers' promotional activity is critical for measuring success of an advertisement. In sales promotion, tracking is also used. For instance, grocery retailers, whose customers are in possession of loyalty cards, have the ability to match customer sales data to coupon use. This information can then be sold to coupon marketers who may use the information to get a better picture of the buying patterns of those responding to the coupon.

### INTERNET COMMUNICATION

For many years consumers typically became aware of sales promotions in passive ways. That is, most customers obtained promotions not through an active search but by being a recipient of a marketer's promotion activity (e.g., received coupons in the mail). The Internet is changing how customers obtain promotions. In addition to websites that offer access to coupons, there are a large number of community forum sites where members share details about how to obtain good deals which often include information on how or where to find a sales promotion. Monitoring these sites may offer marketers insight into how customers feel about certain promotions and may even suggest ideas for future sales promotions.

### CLUTTER AND NEED FOR CREATIVITY

In the same way an advertisement competes with other ads for customers' attention, so to do sales promotions. This is particularly an issue with inserted coupon promotions that may be included in mailing or printed media along with numerous other offerings. The challenge facing marketers is to find creative ways to separate their promotions from those offered by their competitors.

All advertising efforts are directed mainly towards the achievement of business, marketing and advertising objectives (i.e) to increase the sales turnover and thus to market the maximum profit,. The advertiser spends lakhs of rupees in to this advertising activity. In the background of all these efforts, is an attempt to attract the customer towards the product through advertising

In order to measure the effectiveness of advertising copy, two types of tests – pretests and post tests can be undertaken.

Pretests are generally conducted in the beginning of the creation process or at the end of creation process or production stage. There are several pre and posttests techniques to measure the effectiveness of the advertising copy.

The effectiveness of advertising in a particular media may also be measured in any, of the following ways-

(*a*) By giving different addresses to different media.

(*b*) Different newspapers may be selected for advertisements of different departments.

(*c*) Coupon blank etc, may be provided with the advertisement or

(*d*) Enquiry from consumers should mention the name of the source of information. The technique is known as keying the advertising.

Thus in measuring the effectiveness of advertising we include measuring of the effectiveness of advertising campaign, advertising copy and the effectiveness of individual media.

## REVIEW QUESTIONS

1. What is sales promotion
2. State the classification of sales promotion
3. What is consumer sales promotion?
4. What is promotional policy?
5. What is trade in promotion?
6. What are loyalty programmes?
7. Explain various consumer sales promotional measures.
8. How the effectiveness of advertising media can be measured !
9. What are the obectives of sales promotion ?
10. What are contests of sweep stakes!
11. What are various trade sales promotion measurers ?
12. What are trade shows?

# 16 Personal Selling

Personal selling is oral communication with potential buyers of a product with the intention of making a sale. The personal selling may focus initially on developing a relationship with the potential buyer, but will always ultimately end with an attempt to "close the sale"

Personal selling is one of the oldest forms of promotion. It involves the use of a sales force to support a push strategy (encouraging intermediaries to buy the product) or a pull strategy (where the role of the sales force may be limited to supporting retailers and providing after-sales service).

## KOTLER DESCRIBES SIX MAIN ACTIVITIES OF A SALES FORCE:

(1) Prospecting - trying to find new customers

(2) Communicating - with existing and potential customers about the product range

(3) Selling - contact with the customer, answering questions and trying to close the sale

(4) Servicing - providing support and service to the customer in the period up to delivery and also post-sale

(5) Information gathering - obtaining information about the market to feedback into the marketing planning process

(6) Allocating - in times of product shortage, the sales force may have the power to decide how available stocks are allocated

### Advantages of using personal selling as a means of promotion

- Personal selling is a face-to-face activity; customers therefore obtain a relatively high degree of personal attention
- The sales message can be customized to meet the needs of the customer
- The two-way nature of the sales process allows the sales team to respond directly and promptly to customer questions and concerns
- Personal selling is a good way of getting across large amounts of technical or other complex product information
- The face-to-face sales meeting gives the sales force chance to demonstrate the product
- Frequent meetings between sales force and customer provide an opportunity to build good long-term relationships

**Given that there are many advantages to personal selling, why do more businesses not maintain a direct sales force?**

**Main disadvantages of using personal selling:**

The main disadvantage of personal selling is the cost of employing a sales force. Sales people are expensive. In addition to the basic pay package, a business needs to provide incentives to achieve sales (typically this is based on commission and/or bonus arrangements) and the equipment to make sales calls (car, travel and subsistence costs, mobile phone etc).

In addition, a sales person can only call on one customer at a time. This is not a cost-effective way of reaching a large audience.

## PROMOTION - INTRODUCTION TO THE PROMOTIONAL MIX

It is not enough for a business to have good products sold at attractive prices. To generate sales and profits, the benefits of products have to be communicated to customers. In marketing, this is commonly known as "promotion".

## PROMOTION IS ALL ABOUT COMPANIES COMMUNICATING WITH CUSTOMERS

A business' total marketing communications programme is called the "promotional mix" and consists of a blend of advertising, personal selling, sales promotion and public relations tools. In this revision note, we describe the four key elements of the promotional mix in more detail.

It is helpful to define the four main elements of the promotional mix before considering their strengths and limitations.

### (1) Advertising

Any paid form of non-personal communication of ideas or products is the "prime media": i.e. television, newspapers, magazines, billboard posters, radio, cinema etc. Advertising is intended to persuade and to inform. The two basic aspects of advertising are the message (what you want your communication to say) and the medium (how you get your message across)

### (2) Personal Selling

Oral communication with potential buyers of a product is with the intention of making a sale. The personal selling may focus initially on developing a relationship with the potential buyer, but will always ultimately end with an attempt to "close the sale".

### (3) Sales Promotion

Providing incentives to customers or to the distribution channel to stimulate demand for a product.

### (4) Publicity

The communication of a product, brand or business by placing information about it in the media without paying for the time or media space directly. It is otherwise known as "public relations" or PR.

## REVIEW QUESTIONS

1. What do you mean by Personal Selling?
2. What are the main activities of a Sales force?
3. State the merits of using personal selling as a means of promotion.
4. What are the four documents of promotional mix?

# 17 Public Relations

Of the four promotional mix options available to marketers public relations (PR) is probably the least understood and, consequently, often receives the least amount of attention. Many marketers see public relations as only handling rudimentary communication activities, such as issuing press releases and responding to questions from the news media. But in reality, in a time when customers are inundated with thousands of promotional messages everyday, public relations offers powerful methods for cutting through the clutter.

In Part 16 of our highly detailed Principles of Marketing tutorial we see how public relations is growing in importance as a marketing tool and is now a critical component in helping marketers reach their objectives. We will see that PR uses a variety of methods to enhance the relationship between organizations and its target audience. And we will show that when handled correctly PR can allow a marketer's message to raise above other promotional methods.

## WHAT ARE PUBLIC RELATIONS?

Public relations involve the cultivation of favourable relations for organizations and products with its key publics through the use of a variety of communications channels and tools. Traditionally, this meant public relations professionals would work with members of the news media to build a favourable image by publicizing the organization or product through stories in print and broadcast media. But today the role of public relations is much broader and includes:

- Building awareness and a favourable image for a company or client within stories and articles found in relevant media outlets
- Closely monitoring numerous media channels for public comment about a company and its products
- Managing crises that threaten company or product image
- Building goodwill among an organization's target market through community, philanthropic and special programmes and events

In this chapter most of our focus is on how public relations supports marketing by building product and company image (sometimes referred to as publicity). Yet, it should be noted that there are other stakeholders companies reached via the public relations function, such as employees and non-target market groups. Favourable media coverage about a company or product often reaches these audiences as well and may offer potential benefit to the marketer.

Finally, in most large companies, investor relations (IR) or financial public relations is a speciality in itself guided by specific disclosure regulations. However, coverage of this type of PR will not be provided here.

## ADVANTAGES OF PR

Public relations offers several advantages not found with other promotional options. First, PR is often considered a highly credible form of promotion. One of PR's key points of power rests with helping to establish credibility for a product, company or person (e.g., CEO) in the minds of targeted customer groups by capitalizing on the influence of a third-party — the media. Audiences view many media outlets as independent-party sources that are unbiased in their coverage, meaning that the decision to include the name of the company and the views expressed about the company is not based on payment (i.e., advertisement) but on the media outlet's judgment of what is important. For example, a positive story about a new product in the business section of a local newspaper may have greater impact on readers than a full-page advertisement for the product since readers perceive the news media as presenting an impartial perspective of the product.

Second, a well-structured PR campaign can result in the target market being exposed to more detailed information than they receive with other forms of promotion. That is, media sources often provide more space and time for explanation of a product.

Third, depending on the media outlet, a story mentioning a company may be picked up by a large number of additional media, thus, spreading a single story to many locations.

Finally, in many cases public relations objectives can be achieved at very low cost when compared to other promotional efforts. This is not to suggest public relations is not costly, it may be, especially when a marketer hires PR professionals to handle the work. But when compared to the direct cost of other promotions, in particular advertising, the return on promotional expense can be quite high.

## DISADVANTAGES OF PR

While public relations hold many advantages for marketers, there are also concerns using this promotional technique. First, while public relations uses many of the same channels as advertising, such as newspapers, magazines, radio, TV and Internet, it differs significantly from advertising in that marketers do not have direct control over whether a message is delivered and where it is placed for delivery. For instance, a marketer may spend many hours talking with a magazine writer, who is preparing an industry story, only to find that their company is never mentioned in the article.

Second, while other promotional messages are carefully drafted and distributed as written through a pre-determined placement in a media vehicle, public relations generally conveys information to a member of the news media (e.g., reporter) who then redrafts the information as part of a news story or feature. Thus, the final message may not be precisely what the marketer planned.

Third, while a PR campaign has the potential to yield a high return on promotional expense, it also has the potential to produce the opposite if the news media feels there is little value in running a story pitched (i.e., suggested via communication with the news outlet) by the marketer.

Fourth, with PR there is always a chance that a well devised news event or release will get "bumped" from planned media coverage because of a more critical breaking news story, such as wars, severe weather or serious crime.

Finally, in some areas of the world the impact of traditional news outlets is fading forcing public relations professionals to scramble to find new ways to reach their target markets.

## OBJECTIVES OF PUBLIC RELATIONS

Like other aspects of marketing promotion, public relations are used to address several broad objectives including:

- Building Product Awareness – When introducing a new product or relaunching an existing product, marketers can use a PR element that generates consumer attention and awareness through media placements and special events.
- Creating Interest – Whether a PR placement is a short product article or is included with other products in "round up" article, stories in the media can help entice a targeted audience to try the product. For example, around the holiday season, a special holiday food may be promoted with PR through promotional releases sent to the food media or through special events that sample the product.
- Providing Information – PR can be used to provide customers with more in depth information about products and services. Through articles, collateral materials, newsletters and websites, PR delivers information to customers that can help them gain understanding of the product.
- Stimulating Demand – A positive article in a newspaper, on a TV news show or mentioned on the Internet, often results in a discernable increase in product sales.
- Reinforcing the Brand – In many companies the public relations function is also involved with brand reinforcement by maintaining positive relationships with key audiences, and thereby aiding in building a strong image. Today it is ever more important for companies and brands to build a good image. A strong image helps the company build its business and it can help the company in times of crisis as well.

## PUBLIC RELATIONS TOOLS

Marketers should be aware of the tools used in the public relations function. While some marketers may prefer to handle their own PR tasks, many others will seek the assistance of outside PR professionals rather than attempt to handle these activities themselves. Skilled PR professionals offer many advantages for marketers with their two most important things things: (1) their ability to understand and unearth good stories about a company and its product, and (2) their knowledge of the media market may place them in a better position to match stories to the news angles media reporters look for.

Whether handling PR internally or hiring professionals, marketers should be familiar with the tools available for public relations: Before choosing among the various tools marketers should begin by identifying their key targeted audiences (e.g., target markets) and key messages they wish to send. These should align with the messages and audiences identified for the product being promoted or corporate goals for non-specific product promotions, such as corporate image promotions.

The key messages are used in the development of public relations materials and supporting programmes are described below. The purpose of key messages is to provide a consistent point of view over time and across numerous PR methods that reinforce product positioning (i.e., customer's perceptions) and reach the desired target audience.

The key tools available for PR include:

- Media Relations
- Media Tours
- Newsletters
- Special Events
- Speaking Engagements
- Sponsorships
- Employee Relations
- Community Relations and Philanthropy

**Media Relations**

Historically the core of public relations, media relations, includes all efforts to publicise products or the company to members of the press — TV and Radio, newspaper, magazine, newsletter and Internet. In cornering media coverage, PR professionals work with the media to place stories about products, companies and company spokespeople. This is done by developing interesting and relevant story angles that are pitched to the media. It is important to remember that media placements come with good stories and no payment is made to the media for placements. In fact, in order to maintain the highest level of credibility, many news organizations bar reporters from accepting even the smallest gifts (e.g., free pencils with product logo) from companies.

**Key tools used in media relations include:**

- Press Kits - Include written information such as a news release, organization background, key spokesperson biographies and other supporting materials that provide information useful to reporters.
- Audio or Video News Releases - These are prerecorded features distributed to news media that may be included within media programming. For instance, a local news report about amusement parks may include portions of a video news release from a national amusement park company.
- Matte Release - Some media, especially small local newspapers, may accept articles written by companies often as filler material when their publication lacks sufficient content. PR professionals submit matte releases through syndicated services (i.e., services that supply content to many media outlets) or directly to targeted media via email, fax or snail mail.
- Website Press Room - While hard copies of materials are used and preferred by some media, marketers are well served by an online press room that caters to media needs and provides company contact information.

As PR people know, many story ideas for newspapers, magazines and television news often start with a suggestion from a PR person. If things work out, a reporter or editor will, at best, write a positive story with the company as a key feature or, at minimum, include the company's name somewhere within an industry-focused article.

**Media Tours**

Some new products can be successfully publicised when launched with a media tour. On a media tour a company spokesperson travels to key cities to introduce a new product by being booked on TV and radio talk shows and conducting interviews with print and Internet reporters or influencers (e.g., bloggers). The spokesperson can be a company employee or someone hired by the company, perhaps a celebrity or "expert" who has credibility with the target audience. One common use of the media tour is the book tour, where an author travels the country to promote a newly released book. A media tour may include other kinds of personal appearances in conjunction with special events, such as public appearances, speaking engagements or autograph signing opportunities.

### Newsletters

Marketers who have captured names and addresses of customers and potential customers can use a newsletter for regular contact with their targeted audience. Newsletters can be directed at trade customers, final consumers or business buyers and can be distributed either by regular mail or electronic means (i.e., e-newsletters delivered via email or RSS feed). Marketers using newsletters strive to provide content of interest to customers as well as information on products and promotions. A bookstore may include reviews of new books, information on online book chats and information on in-store or online promotions. A food manufacturer may include seasonal recipes, information on new products and coupons. Online newsletters offer the opportunity to link to a sales page that directs to store carrying product or to a direct online store. Effective newsletters are sought out by and well received by interested audiences.

### Special Events

These run the gamest from receptions to elegant dinners to stunts. Special events can be designed to reach a specific narrow target audience, such as individuals interested in college savings plans to major events like a strawberry festival designed to promote tourism and regional agriculture. Stunts, such as building the world's largest ice cream during National Ice Cream month captures the attention of an audience in the immediate area, but also attracts the attention of mass media such as TV news and major newspapers, which provide broad reach. The Oscar Mayer Weiner mobile is a classic example, providing a recognizable icon that travels the country garthering attention wherever it visits. As with all PR programs, special event planners must work hard to ensure the program planned conveys the correct message and image to the target audience.

### Speaking Engagements

Speaking before industry conventions, trade association meetings, and other groups provides an opportunity for company experts to demonstrate their expertise to potential clients/customers. Generally these opportunities are not explicitly for company or product promotion; rather they are a chance to talk on a topic of interest to potential customers and serve to highlight the speaker's expertise in a field. Often the only mention of the company or its products is in the speaker biography. Nevertheless, the right speaking engagement puts the company in front of a good target audience and offers networking opportunities for generating customer leads.

### Sponsorships

Companies and brands use sponsorships to help build goodwill and brand recognition by associating with an event or group. Marketers can examine sponsorship opportunities to find those that reach target groups, fit within a specified budget and provide sponsorship benefits that suit the marketer's objectives. There are numerous local, regional, national and international sponsorship opportunities ranging from a local art center or theatre to the Olympics. Most organizations seeking company sponsors provide information on the variety of sponsorship levels which include data on event audience, exposure opportunities, which can include signage, T-shirts, public announcements and numerous other opportunities, receptions and much more. Marketers can use this information to help match sponsorship opportunities with the company's objectives.

### Employee Communications

For many companies communicating regularly with employees is important in keeping employees informed of corporate programs, sales incentives, personnel issues, as well as keeping them updated on new products and programs. Companies use a variety of means to communicate with employees, including Intranet, email, online and print newsletters. In larger firms an in-house PR department often works in conjunction with the Human Resources Department to develop employee communications.

### Community Relations and Philanthropy

For many companies fostering good relations with key audiences includes building strong relationships with their regional community. Companies implement programmes supportive of the community ranging from supporting local organizations and institutions (e.g., arts organizations, community activities, parks) to conducting educational workshops (e.g., for teachers, parents) to donating product for community events and charitable fundraisers. The goal is generally to develop a positive relationship with members of the community (i.e., be known as a good neighbor). Effective community relations can help a company whether bad publicity or a crisis situation that can unexpectedly arise due to a problem with a product, unethical behavior by management, or even by false rumours. Some companies also make an effort to contribute to charitable organizations, often organizations that have some relationship to the company's mission or to a key principal of the company.

## ADDITIONAL PR ACTIVITIES

In addition to serving as means for helping to achieve marketing objectives, public relations professionals may undertake additional activities, aimed at maintaining a positive image for an organization. These activities include:

### Market Monitoring

Monitoring public comment about a company and its products is becoming increasingly important especially with the explosion of information channels on the Internet. Today monitoring includes watching what is written and reported in traditional print and broadcast media and also keeping an eye on discussions occurring through various Internet outlets such as forums, chatrooms, blogs and other public messaging areas. Marketers must be prepared to respond quickly to erroneous information and negative opinions about products as it can spin out of control very quickly through the new technology channels. Failure to correct misinformation can be devastating to a product or company's reputation. It should be noted that specialized monitoring services can be contracted to help companies keep track of "buzz" about the company and its products.

### Crisis Management

Marketers need to be prepared to respond quickly to negative information about the company. When a problem with a product arises — in fact or substantiated only by rumor — a marketer's investment in a product and brand can be in serious jeopardy. Today, with the prevalence of the Internet and wireless communications, negative information can spread rapidly. Through monitoring marketers can track the issues and respond in a timely fashion. To manage response effectively, many companies have crises management plans in place that outline steps to take and company spokesperson to speak on behalf of the company, should an event occur.

### Trends in Public Relations

Until recently most public relations activity involved person-to-person contact between PR professionals and members of the media, such as journalists and television news reporters. However, several trends are developing that alter the tasks performed by PR people. In most cases these changes are the result of new Internet technologies that are quickly gaining widespread acceptance among Internet users and are becoming new media outlets in their own right.

## THE IMPORTANT TRENDS IN PUBLIC RELATIONS INCLUDE:

### Voicing Opinion

Developing websites has long been a time-consuming and often overly technical undertaking for the vast majority of marketers. But this changed with the evolution of easier to use site development applications which allow for quick creation and convenient updating of site content. Additionally, the move toward easier to use website software has changed the purpose of having a presence on the Internet. Where previously the main objective of a website was for advertising, delivering information and e-commerce, the web now serves as a platform for people to voice their opinions.

There are two key applications that fall into this category – blogs and forums.

### Blogs

Blogs, short for weblogs, are a phenomenon that shows just how powerful and influential the Internet has become as a communication medium. Millions of blogs are now available and specialized search engines have been developed to search millions of postings.

Blogs may be most famous as a tool for political discussion, but they are also becoming an important communication tool for public relations. Many companies in both technical fields, such as eBay, Google, and Microsoft, and non-technical fields, such as General Motors, McDonalds and Well Fargo Bank, now produce in-house blogs that report on happenings at the company. These blogs allow company employees, including CEOs and marketers, to post messages updating company developments and, thus, serve as useful PR tool.

### Forums

Web forums are the child of the old Internet bulletin board services where people can post their opinion often anonymously. Forums pose both opportunities and threats for those involved in PR. A presence in an influential forum helps build credibility for an organization as forum members recognize a company's effort to reach out to the public. On the other hand, forums can cause major problems as a breeding ground for rumor and accusation. Public relations personnel must continually monitor forums and respond to misguided comments posted on a web discussion board to help squelch rumors before they can catch fire.

### Really Simple Syndication Feeds (RSS)

An important trend for delivering company information is through an Internet technology known by the acronym RSS (what it stands for depends on who you ask but most accepted name is Really Simple Syndication). This technology makes it easy for people to know when new content is posted to a website.

While there are several flavors of RSS, the basic concept has content providers, such as news sites, corporate websites, blogs, etc., creating RSS documents that provide basic details of new content, such as content title, authorship information, description and links to the full content. The nature of the technology allows anyone who links to the RSS feed to instantly receive details of the content. Many journalists and other media members are finding this to be a more convenient way to acquire information, particularly if they follow a specific industry and can identify specific information websites to monitor. By subscribing to relevant RSS feeds they have information delivered rather than spending time searching.

### Pod casting

The emergence of the Apple Pod and other digital audio players has significantly altered how people listen to music by allowing easy downloading of desired songs. But the use of audio players is not limited to music downloads; a fast growing application is to deliver other content including programming. Public relations may soon find pod casting to be a quick and easy way to send out audio news releases and other promotional material.

### Search Engine Optimization

Publicity is about getting media outlets to mention the name of a product, company or person. For several years Internet marketers have recognized the importance of getting their company and products listed in the top rankings in search engines. So called efforts at Search Engine Optimization (SEO) involve concerted efforts and specific techniques to attain higher rankings.

While at first glance SEO may not seem like a responsibility of public relations, it would appear to contain the main characteristics for making it so, namely getting a third-party media outlet (i.e., search engine) to mention the company (i.e., search rankings) at no direct cost the company (i.e., no payment for ranking). And, just as PR people can use methods to affect coverage within traditional media, optimizing a website can work to influence results in search engines by using techniques that allow a website to fit within ever-changing search engine ranking criteria. In this way SEO does what PR professionals do, namely obtain good placement in third-party media outlet. Consequently, SEO may soon become an important PR function.

## REVIEW QUESTIONS

1. What do you mean by Public Relations?
2. What is market motivating?
3. What are Blogs?
4. What are forums?
5. Explain various public relations tools?
6. State the merits and demerits of Public Relations.

# Advertising Management

# 18 Origin and Development of Advertising

## 1. INTRODUCTION

It is a very common term known to the man. The word Advertising is derived from a Latin word 'Advertere' which means to *'Turn Attention towards a specific thing"*. The dictionary meaning of the word advertising is to announce, publicity or to give public notice. The simplest meaning of an advertisement is that it is a public announcement.

It may be interpreted to turn the attention of the people concerned to a specific thing. Which has been announced by the advertiser, publicly in order to inform and to influence them with the new ideas? In this way, advertising is turning the attention of the people towards product, services, and ideas by an identified sponsor.

It is a paid form of non-personal communication of ideas, goods or services to the people by a sponsor or organization. It is a vital tool of marketing of goods, services and ideas. It is intended to influence the prospective consumer in the market and create new customers. It is thus the method or mode of carrying a message to the prospective customer to buy a particular product.

## DEFINITIONS:

American Marketing Association: *"It is any paid form of non personal presentation and promotion of ideas, goods and services by an identified sponsor"*

William.J.Stanton, *"It consists of all the activities involved in presenting to a group, a non-personal, oral or visual, openly sponsored message regarding a product service or ideas"*

Philip Kotler,*"It is non personal form of communication conducted through paid media under clear sponsorship"*

It is personal presentation of ideas goods or services by an identified sponsor for the purpose of inducing the prospects to buy them.

## ORIGIN AND GROWTH OF ADVERTISING

The colourful history of advertising can be divided into six clear cut periods that consist of centuries of growth and developments.

### 1. Ancient Times :

Hammerbi rules in Babylon 2000 year before christ, the artisans, shoemakers, Backers and other merchants were eager to exchange their goods for money, and advertising came to their timely help for selling of goods in ancient times through personal selling activities. Merchants needed to identify their places with a symbol that told their trade and the shop shine were born. The merchants impressed upon the minds of consumers of the qualities of their wares. Other form of communication was the wall signs. Advertisement was affixed on the wall of the tall buildings near-by important places.

**2. Between Fifth to Eighth centuries:**

In this period commerce and trade rules were drastically diminished. Advertising was done either by human voice and/or by hand executed signs and play cards.

**3. Between 9th and 15th Centuries:**

In this period new methods of advertising were available like as printed posters, hand bills, signs, pamphlets, books and newspapers.

**4. Between 16th and 17th Centuries:**

During the 16th century newspapers were available in the printed form. The First news letter was established in 1622 in England. Latter half of the 16th century witnessed newspapers in the form of news books and were come by the middle of 17th century. The outstanding features of 17th century are that there were special advertising periodicals. By 1675, Newspapers were published. By the end of 17th century newspapers were well established in England undertaking on a regular basis.

**5. Between 18th and 19th centuries:**

The 19th century was marked by a new trend of brand advertising. Magazines – both weeklies and monthlies started for catching the imagination of the people by popularizing the brands. In this period, the window and counter display and trade fairs are arranged for effective advertisement.

**6. 20th Century:**

The current 20th century is marked with the advent of two fascinating media of communication namely, Radio and Television. Americans have the credit of having these first. Radio rules the scene from 1922 to 1947 and 1948 onwards the television took over.

Radio advertising has an edge over print publicity that it is capable of reaching the millions of illiterate people as it is voice advertising. Television could beat radio advertising with the visual effects. Television has been powerful means of advertising since 1950 and has grown in importance with its colour effects, and is going to rule for few more decades to come. These are the major indoor powerful media, The outdoor advertising has its own developments, such as traveling displays, nionsigns, skywriting in addition to the earlier means like posters, printed display and sandwich man.

## DEVELOPMENT OF ADVERTISING

The speedy development of advertising was accelerated on account of the following factors.

- The industrial production led to mass production on account of advanced machines and the need of advertising for selling the same.
- With the development of improved means of transport and communication. Advertising gain the needed communication vehicle for contact with the consumers.
- Increasing literacy was also responsible for the development of advertising media
- With the increase in literacy rate, the number of newspapers and magazines were increased. They carried the message about the new products to consumers.
- The advent and development of advertising agency in the beginning of the 20th century give impetus (Trade between two countries) to the rapid development of advertising.

- The current century marked with the advent of Radio, Television, Telephone etc., added impetus to the development of advertising. And now one step more the colour transmission has made advertising more attractive

## REVIEW QUESTIONS:

1. Define Advertising
2. Discuss the factors that are present for development of advertising.

# 19 Legal Framework of Advertising

Government, almost in every country, controls or regulates the business. In India the government has shown a keen interest in how the businesses are run since independence. The governmental rules and regulations define in most of the cases how firms are to prepare their financial and profit and loss statements; they have limited the borrowing powers of the business; and through regulatory commissions they specify the way a firm can conduct its profit making activities.

Advertising is an integral part of modern life and its persuasive ability has a large impact on society. It has a large responsibility with in our economic system and is a highly visible and institution affecting many people. But it injuries the buyer and the economy if the advertisement is deceptive. Deceptive advertisement means when the information provided in the advertisement is misleading, deceptive, manipulative or undesirable. It represents an unethical behaviour of the businessman that has unfortunate effects on consumers ranging from misspent money on an item that did not live up to the expectations developed in the advertising to hazardous accidents resulting from the mis-representation of faulty goods.

Three major institutions are there in the society that protects consumers against mis-leading or fraudulent advertising.

A. Government agencies enforcing laws against offenders

B. Advertising industry associations and media groups that impose self regulation upon their member firms and advertisers

C. Advertisers themselves are acting through enlightened self-interest and a sense of social responsibility.

Advertising is self-publicizing. The content of advertising message is a matter of public record. Competitors and consumers both are in good position to expose the dishonest or misleading advertising. It is therefore, good if the business imposes the self regulation upon them and not to publish only advertisement that contains a false statement whatsoever. Advertisers should realize that truthful advertising, leading to consumer satisfaction, is the only successful long range strategy to follow. Developing loyal customers through misleading ads is difficult, if not impossible. Therefore, enlightened companies establish their own guidelines designed to ensure that their advertising does not violate the general rules of honesty and fair play.

Advertising industry association and the individual firms should impost self-regulations upon their members and themselves. They should be honest in their trade and should not accept the advertisements containing misleading or deceptive statements because they also have certain social responsibility towards customers and society. If what they are doing is not in pur suit of their careers in the advertising business, is not up to the standards of our society, their lives will contain undesirable frustration.

## RECOMMENDATIONS OF SACHAR COMMITTEE

The Sachar Committee has recommended the following acts of sellers as unfair trade practice.

1. Misleading advertisements and false representation – A seller should not falsely represent that
   (*a*) the goods are of a particulars standards, quality, grade composition, style or model, if they do not possess that qualification;
   (*b*) the rebuilt, second hand goods are new goods.
2. Offering of gifts or prizes with the intention of not providing them and conducting professional contests.

The committee is of the opinion that all the aforesaid unfair trade practices should be punishable as an offence or any person or undertaking indulging in any of these activities should be liable to be prosecuted before the commission.

## SELF-REGULATION OF ADVERTISING

Advertising people have long been committed to the idea of self regulation. The foundation for legislation against deceptive advertising was passed by the state legislature largely through the job buying efforts of advertising clubs throughout the nation. Several other non-legislative efforts of the advertising industry were made in its efforts to keep its own house clean.

In 1971, an ambitious programme of self regulation was established by the Advertising club of Cleveland, Ohio of advertising industry in concert with the Council of Better Business Bureaus (CBBB). The objectives of such programme were to establish a self regulatory mechanism that would respond constructively to public complaints about national advertising and would significantly improve advertising performance and credibility. It was further intended that this mechanism be flexible, different, respected and reliable. The programme was initially started to be concerned with matters of truth and accuracy in advertising and to avoid deception and false advertising but has expanded its interests to include the broader questions of taste and social responsibility. The following are the outlines of the programme.

Complaints against National Advertising Division (NAD), an arm of CBBB. In evaluating a complaint NAD normally request the advertiser for substantiation for the claims made in the challenged advertisement. Following its investigation the NAD (i) if finds the complaint correct and justified, will request the advertiser to modify or with draw the challenged advertising, or (ii) it may dismiss the claim on the ground that the advertiser, in NAD's opinion, provided adequate substantiation of his claims.

Any decision of the NAD is appeal able. Either the advertiser or the complainant, who disagrees with the decision may appeal to the National Advertising Review Board (NARB) consisting of a chairman and 50 other members from the advertisers, agencies and from outside the industry. In response to the appeal, the chairman at his discretion may appoint a five member panel to review the case. If finding of the panel are in favour of the advertiser, the case if filed is closed. If, not the advertiser will be asked to modify or discontinue the advertisement under review. If the advertiser refuses to modify or discontinue the advertisement as directed by NARB, the case in referred by the NARB to an appropriate government agency. Public disclosure is made of the findings of all NARB panels, together with any statement submitted by the advertiser in his support.

The self regulation technique, as said earlier is on the lines of council of Better Business Bureaus. Today over 240 of such bureaus operate in USA both at local and national level to fight illegal and deceptive advertising and to raise the advertising standards. Advertiser, advertising agencies and advertising media work together to stamp out deep time advertising. Through BBB approach, each Bureau acts as a watchdog within its community. The effectiveness of bureaus varies greatly from city to city. This is due to quality of leadership operating as local unit and the amount of fundamental and other support provided to the bureaus.

## REVIEW QUESTIONS

1. What are the three major institutions that protect consumers against misleading advertisement?
2. What are the recommendations made by Sachar Committee?
3. How advertising can be self regulated?

# 20 OBJECTIVES OF ADVERTISING

## INTRODUCTION

The main purpose of the business is to serve the society by fulfilling the needs of customers. Firms to maintain it economically sound; must generate sales that yield long run profits. Advertising may contribute to sales. Thus the main purpose of advertising is to generate sales and increase profits of the firm and all other objectives will be achieved automatically.

The real objective of advertising is effective communication between producers and consumers. In other words, the ultimate objective underlying all advertising is to increase the awareness. It aims at committing the education to the consumers, supplementing the salesman, connecting the dealer to eliminate the competitor; It is a link between the producer and the consumer.

## MAIN OBJECTIVES OF ADVERTISING

- Preparation of ground for sale of new product
- Creation of demand
- Educating the consumers and the users
- Building up brand image and brand loyalty
- Facing competition'
- Informing about the changes to the consumers and the users
- Neutralizing competitors advertising
- Enhancing goodwill of the firm
- Performing selling job
- Assisting salesman's effort
- Reduction in production and distribution cost
- Maintenance of demand

## MATHEW, BUZZLE AND FRANK'S ADVERTISING OBJECTIVES ARE:-

- To make an immediate sale
- To build primary market
- To introduce a price deal
- To inform about product availability
- To build brand recognition or brand insistence
- To help to the salesman by building an awareness of a product among retailers
- To create a reputation for service, reliability or research strength
- To increase market share

- To modify the existing product appeals and product motives
- To inform about the availability of new products or features or price
- To increase the frequency use of a product
- To increase the number or quality of retail outlets.
- To build over all company image
- To create immediate buying action
- To reach new areas or new segments of population and to develop overseas

**The objectives are mainly classified into**

(I) General Objectives

(II) Specific Objectives

## GENERAL OBJECTIVES

The general objectives are those that are followed by every company. They may be called main or primary objectives. It is nothing but to sell something – a product, a service or an idea. A firm accomplishes this purpose by maintaining an effective communication between the firm and consumers.

The general objectives may be classified into two, they are

### (a) Stimulating Demand:

Advertising can stimulate the demand for any product in three basic ways.

(*i*) The present users of product may be persuaded to increase the present rate of product consumption. This may be done by reminding the present users about the product and its brand and the possible advantages of using such products.

(*ii*) The second way of stimulating demand for the product is to attract new users into the market by telling them the qualities of the product and its possible users, so that they may change their brand.

(*iii*) The third possible way of stimulating is to tell the present users about the new users of the product. so that the customer may use the company for many other purposes. In this way advertising may bring new areas and customers to the companies' product and thus stimulate for it.

### (b) Increased Profits:

Advertising may affect the profit performance of the business firm in two important ways.

(*i*) Advertising increase the sales of the product. The increase in sales will result in mass scale of production and thus it may favourably affect the product cost. Manufacturing cost will be lower. The profits of the concern will be increased consequently.

(*ii*) Similarly advertising will reduce the various marketing cost. Increased advertisement will require less expenditure on personal selling, less per unit cost on transportation and storage due to increased sales. Thus advertising increases profits of concern due to reduction in manufacturing and marketing costs.

## SPECIFIC OBJECTIVES

The advertisement is specifically used for the following purposes.

**1. Preparing ground for new product**

Advertising may be used when a new product or service is being introduced by manufacturers. New product needs introduction because prospective buyers have never used it and advertising prepares a ground for new product. Presenting full details to new consumers about the products involves high cost because it needs comprehensive details and frequent appearance of gained advertisement in news papers and posters colours to attract the attention of the prospective users.

**2. Facing competition**

Another important objective of advertising is to face the competition in the market. Advertising in modern days is used not only to inform the people about a new or existing product but it is also used to maintain and increase the demand of the product by keeping people away from rival's products available in the market. Under competitive conditions, advertising creates brand image and brand loyalty. So the customers develop a habit to use the product.

**3. Informing the changes to the consumers**

The advertisement is made with the purpose of informing to the consuming public. whenever changes are made in prices, channels of distribution or in the product by way of any improvement in quality, size, weight, brand, packing etc. They are informed to the public through advertisement.

**4. Neutralizing Competition**

When competitors adopt new and intensive advertising as their promotional strategy, advertising basically helps to create product differentiation by particular message and creates image.

**5. Barring new entrants**

Advertiser creates an image through repetitive advertising. It helps to keep new entrants away. The regular advertising builds up certain type of monopoly of the product in the market and the new entrant finds its difficult to enter into the market until it faces new challenges. So advertising keeps the new competitors off the market.

**6. Creating Goodwill**

Advertising is often undertaken with the objective of creating goodwill for the producers. This in turn increases the market receptiveness of the consumer's products and helps to the sales man to win consumer easily.

**7. To assist salesman**

Advertisement creates a positive image in the minds of prospective customers. Some companies with large fields of sales force, believe that a whole advertisement will act as a moral booster of such sales force because advertising makes the job of the sales man easier.

**8. To expand the market to new buyers**

One of the purposes of advertising is to expand the market for the consumer's product in any one of the following ways.

(*i*) Having been used the product successfully for industrial or commercial purposes; its use may be promoted to consumers through advertisement.

(*ii*) Some times company provides special offers to attract new customers due to various reasons like slack season, policy to expand sales etc., (*iii*) Advertiser generally invites enquires from business man to acquire the business and despatch tariffs, price list and branches in response to these queries and conduct the business by post. Thus advertising finds new customers in this way.

(*iv*) In order to have an easy access to customers, the manufacturers open their retail stores or appoint stockist of their products in various places.

Thus advertising in all the above cases helps in expanding the market to new consumers.

### 9. Reminding customers

There are products which are bought very frequently – usually small units like tea, coffee, general merchandise etc. and reminder advertising aims to remind the customers to purchase the same product again and again. In such cases brand names are made popular.

### 10. Other purposes

**The following are certain other objectives of advertising**

(*i*) For seeking staff – skilled, unskilled, semi skilled or professional for higher positions. Such advertisement also says some thing about the employer and the terms and conditions of employment.

(*ii*) Some advertisement for raising funds by public companies, govt., or govt. undertakings etc. informs the general public about the nature of investment.

(*iii*) The another form of financial advertising is to announce trading results through news papers, radio and television. It helps to increase the growth of concern.

(*iv*) It plays an important role in the life of manufacturing units. It aims at the benefits of producers, educating the consumer and supplementing the salesman.

## SETTING OF ADVERTISING OBJECTIVES

The following are the elements which are to be considered in setting an objective

### 1. Sales as an objective

A convenient advertising involves constructing of sales or market share. The immediate aim of advertising is often to raise the level of sales.

### 2. Operational objectives

Where immediate sales preciously form the basis of operation and objectives, the ultimate behavior of advertising is attempting to re-enforce the nature of the determinants of the advertising.

### 3. Behavioral dynamics

An understanding of market dynamics is necessary to analyse the ultimate behaviour of advertising from new consumers attracted for the first time.

(*i*) By increasing the loyalty of existing customers.

(*ii*) By inducing existing customers to use more of the product.

### 4. Behavioral variable

If the advertising target is to get new customers, the goal may be to get new customers to try our brand for the first time. If it were possible to attract new customer largely through advertising they will make the trial purchase and they would provide the basis for an appropriate behavioural objectives.

**5. Specifying the target segments**

Advertising should specify the target audience and how those audiences are to be influenced by the advertisement. The segments can be defined on the basis of customer characteristics like age, income, life style and product.

**6. Multiple objectives**

It could involve more than one target audience. The consumer might gain awareness among one segment and to communicate the existence of a new product in other segments or there may be two communication tasks for the same target segment.

## REVIEW QUESTION

1. State the Main objectives of Advertising.
2. What are the General objectives of advertising?
3. How an advertisement objective can be set?
4. State the specific objectives of advertising.

# 21 DAGMAR APPROACH

In 1961 Russell. H. Colley has distinguished 52 possible advertising objectives in his book *"Defining advertising goals for advertising results"*. He has thus introduced an approach, known after the book title ad Dagmar Approach to advertising planning and induced a precise method for turning advertising objectives into specific measurable goals. In addition the performance could be measured later against these goals to see whether they have been achieved. The general concept developed in Dagmar Approach has received wide recognition that raised certain controversies, with these results. The researchers and behavioral scientist developed several other models contributing to the original Dagmar approach. An advertisement goal is a specific communication task, to be accomplished among a defined audience, in a given period of time.

One possible target for advertising may be fixed in terms of the number of potential customers. Then the number of customers attracted by the brand name. An attempt is also made to develop or maintain the loyalty of existing customers. The loyalty of customers towards the brand is to be increased only by improving product image or maintaining awareness level.

Advertising may also increase the product usage for the existing customers. This approach is to set a refinement and extension of Dagmar Approach.

## GENERAL SUGGESTIONS ON IMPLEMENTATION

The Dagmar approach was not very specific in its advice to the persons charged with its implementation. One suggestion was that a systematic information gathering process, termed the 6 M's approach be employed to analyze the market and product situation. Another suggestion was to use a checklist of reasonable promotional task

## THE 6 M APPROACH

Merchandise

Markets

Messages

Motives

Media

Measurements

### Merchandise

It evaluates the strength and weaknesses of the product and analyse the benefit offered by the product in comparison to the competitors' product. Any differential advertisement should be noted.

### Markets

This analysis involves the present and past users of the product and the intermediaries distributing it and one objective of this analysis is to identify the alternative segmentation strategies. The effect on intermediaries should also be considered because its place is a very important one in influencing the market.

### Motives

In order to gain understanding some facts above motives should be analyzed such as why do people buy? What rationale and emotional reason for purchase decision? What motives are involved? What are relevant consumption system with which imbedded? What are the goals of this consumption system? The answers to these questions should be considered for decision making.

### Message

What alternative appeals could influence prospective consumer to purchase? What appeals have been used in the past?. The appeal should be different from the present and past appeals of competitors?

### Media

In media analysis, different media should be evaluated on the basis of advantages, constrain and suitability to the advisor and the product. They can interact meaningfully with the segment selected and appeal used.

### Measurement

It refers to the measures that are needed to be obtained during this audit state, not only to provide benchmark to measure future progress but also to provide guidance in establishing objectives.

Another suggestion, to those implementing Dagmar approach is checklist of promotional task. Check list contained several questions with their suggestions. Each of the promotional tasks should be rated in terms of its relative context of product situation involved. Again the intent was to stimulate ideas or decisions offend.

## REVIEW QUESTIONS

1. What is Dagmar Approach?
2. Explain the concept of 6 M Approach.

# 22 NATURE OF ADVERTISING

It is a non personal paid method of mass communication which is aimed at promoting ideas, goods and services by an identified sponsor. It is done by the commercial and non commercial organization. It is gaining importance at a very rapid speed in different sectors of economy i.e. why it is being used both by the public and private sector. The communication in advertising is very speedy, in permitting an advertiser to speak to millions of prospective customers in a few hours.

**1. Advertising is an Art :**

It has been recognized as an art because the creative function of advertising is very much depending upon the creativity of the individual. The creation of the copy of advertisement includes its message, theme, design, layout, use of combination of colour, symbols, pictures, illustrations etc. The individual capacity and an instinct of creating always something new are the essence of advertising. In this way advertising is an art.

**2. Advertising as a science :**

It is a developing science, where the study of planning, organizing and decision making is undertaken. Various principles, techniques, methods, strategies of advertising are developing as per needs of the society. With the study of these techniques, a successful and effective advertising is progressing. Different media of advertising are developed at a very fast speed.

**3. Advertising is persuasive :**

The major aim of advertisement is to attract the consumers. In this sense it is persuasive to buy a certain product at a certain price from specified places. It is an inevitable campaign of industrialization. It finds the market and keep the wheels of the industry turning by maintaining constant demand of the product. The persuasive aspect of advertising must perform the following five functions. They are

- To attract attention of the viewers
- To command interest
- To create desire
- To inspire conviction
- To provoke action

**4. Advertising is multi-purpose:**

It is multi-purpose. It is done by commercial and non commercial organizations, political and non political organizations, social and non social organizations and groups and individuals.

## SCOPE OF ADVERTISING

- Evaluation and development of different media of advertising
- Selection of suitable advertising media in accordance with the nature of product and size as well as field of the enterprise which can stimulate the sales amongst the present and prospective customer.
- Mass communication to the consumers, users, manufacturers etc.
- Providing support to the dealers, distributors, wholesalers and sales force.
- Maintenance and development of brand image and loyalty amongst the customers which also develops loyalty to the enterprise.
- Promoting the overall image of trust, confidence, and respect for the organization amongst those who are closely related with the enterprise such as shareholders, creditors, government, customers and the general public.
- Increasing the area of advertising from local to regional, national and international fields.

## CHARACTERISTICS OR ELEMENTS OF ADVERTISING :

- It is non personal communication to specific audience or consumers
- It is a paid form of communication by an identified sponsor.
- It may be visual, spoken, oral or written
- Disseminate information on products or services to the consumers
- It presents the message about products' availability in the market
- It persuades people to buy a product by creating interest
- It is the promotion of ideas, goods and services
- It supplements the voice and personality of individual salesman. It is salesmanship in print.
- It is a general term used for any and all types of publicity
- It is essential to inform the customer through different media about the product and its features.
- It stimulates sales for the product
- It helps indirectly for positioning the product in the market
- It carries the message of the manufacturer or the seller to the target audience
- It is an essential form of communication for introducing a new product in the market.

## FUNCTIONS OF ADVERTISING

It can be classified into Primary Functions and Secondary functions.

### I. Primary Functions :

- To assist the dealers
- To increase the sales
- To persuade the dealers
- To remove the obstacles to sales
- To develop brand preference
- To increase per capita income

- To secure initial attention
- To provide insurance
- To eliminate seasonal fluctuations
- To raise standard of living of the customers

**II. Secondary Functions:**

- To assist sales man and boost their morale
- To furnish the required information to the wholesalers, middlemen, salesmen and retailers etc.,
- To increase profits by increasing sales
- To assist the enterprise
- To reduce production and selling cost
- To increase the confidence and morale of the workers

**III. Commercial Functions**

From the practical point of view, commercial functions mean to stimulate the sale of goods and services. Increased sales may be accomplished by selling the goods to more people or by selling in greater quantity to people who are already consuming that particular product or new customers or by both, Advertisings creates a favourable climate towards the goods which facilitate sales.

Advertising stimulates demand, develop the brand preferences, to keep old customers, to attracts new customers, introduces new uses of product, helps the dealers, sales men, the prospective customers etc. Advertising helps in eliminating seasonal fluctuations in demand.

**IV. Economic Functions:**

Advertising is productive since

- It provides necessary information to consumers so as to satisfy his wants
- It gives the consumers a feeling of safety that he is purchasing right products
- It tends to stabilize prices
- It helps in bringing down the prices
- It enables the consumer to satisfy more wants and thus increase his standard of living
- It enables large scale productions by widening the extent of the market for goods
- It increases the profits of the enterprise
- It helps in reducing cost of production and distribution

**V. Psychological functions:**

1. To create initial attention to consumers. Every advertiser is supposed to be an matured psychologist
2. To secure initial attention of the prospective buyer, through the use of mechanical devices such as contrast, size position, arrangements, colour, Isolation from competing appeals.
3. To impel action for buying it. This is achieved through vivid appeals to wants, desire and impel.
4. To direct actions in desired channels

5. To develop brand loyalty.
6. To raise standard of living of public

### VI. Social Functions:

Advertising touches the life of people quite intimately. It

- Makes the people happier, healthier and better citizens.
- Helps to remove the diseases and overcome ignorance and illiteracy
- Makes more popular and universal the use of inventions such as automobiles, Radio, Television, Tape recorders and Household appliances.

### VII. Miscellaneous Functions :

- It increases the per capita use of the product by constant reputation of advertisements.
- It helps the enterprise to secure better employees, executive, salesman, workers etc
- It increases the confidence and morale of the workers by developing the feeling that they are working in a reputed enterprise where their jobs are not only secured but also have wide promotion amenities.
- It assists the salesman in increasing sales and boost up their morale.

## PRINCIPLES OF ADVERTISING OR ESSENTIAL ELEMENTS OF GOOD ADVERTISING:

According to R.H.Bushkrick, *"The main principle of an effective advertising is that it reaches the targeted audience at right time with the right message along with right media"*.

1. Know your prospects given before giving advertising. The advertisement should be made in accordance to the level of education, standard income, culture, needs and social customs.
2. The advertisement should create interest in the minds of the prospects towards the products.
3. The advertisement should have attractive head lines. It should create sensation in the minds of the prospects.
4. It should be easily understandable.
5. It should prove the product value.
6. It should attract the prospects using coloured pictures.
7. Demonstrate the novelty of your product.
8. It must be creative.
9. The prospect should feel pride in having the product.
10. Others:
    (*i*) Service element
    (*ii*) Quality element
    (*iii*) In accordance to the time, place and others.
    (*iv*) Convincing
    (*v*) Understand the problems of prospects and their solution.

## REVIEW QUESTIONS:

1. Discuss the scope of advertising.
2. State the essential elements of good advertising
3. Explain the functions of advertising
4. State the Characteristics of advertising.

# 23 TYPES OF ADVERTISING

## GENERAL TYPES

### 1. Persuasive Advertising:

This kind of advertising persuades people to buy those things which they do not want. It finds the market and keeps the wheel of the industry turning by maintaining demand. The persuasive advertising should perform the following five functions, namely

- Attract attention
- Command interest
- Create desire
- Inspire conviction
- Provoke action

### 2. Product Advertising :

When advertising is done with a view to promoting the sale of a particular product, it is called product advertising. This type of advertising is intended to inform the market about a particular product. It is a most common type of advertisement. The object behind product advertising is to create demand of the particular type of product. It may be direct action advertising or indirect action advertising or delayed action advertising.

In direct action advertising, the advertiser wants a quick response for his advertising. The buyer is urged to take an immediate step as to buy the particular product.

Indirect or delayed advertising is intended to stimulate demand of particular product over long a period of time and also by creating awareness on the part of the consumer.

Product advertising may further be classified as primary demand advertising or selective demand advertising. Primary demand advertising is intended to build up the demand for the entire class of product, selective demand or brand advertising is intended to create the demand of a specific brand of a product.

### 3. Institutional Advertising :

It is designed or aimed to create a proper attitude towards the seller and to build goodwill or image for the advertiser rather than to sell a specific product or service. Most of the companies are successful in making their image in the minds of the people by using their names, such as Bata, Bombay Dying etc,

**4. National Advertising :**

It is sponsored by the manufacturers of the product and is intended to cover a wide market.

**5. Local Advertising:**

It is sponsored by the retailer and is intended to cover the local public or local market only

**6. Consumer Advertising:**

When advertising is directed to attract the consumers who buy for ultimate consumption or use, it is called consumer advertising. The object of this advertising is to create demand for various consumer goods.

**7. Industrial Advertising:**

It is directed to attract the industrial users to purchase the product. The object of this advertising is to create demand for industrial goods which are used by the industry concerned such as tools, spare parts etc.,

**8. Commercial Advertising:**

It is concerned with the increasing the sale of commercial enterprises. It is also called as business advertising. The forms of commercial advertising are,

(a) Industrial advertising

(b) Trade Advertising

(c) Professional advertising

(d) Form Advertising

**9. Non Commercial Advertising:**

It is one which is undertaken by non profit organization such as Government charitable and religious institution to support ideas and raising donations etc

**10. Co-operative Advertising:**

It is undertaken by a group of persons or enterprises on cooperative basis.

**11. Emotional Advertising:**

When appeals are directed to emotional feelings of the customer so as to create demand of a particular product it is called emotional advertising.

**12. Intended Audience Advertising:**

When advertising is undertaken targeting a particular group of product audience it is called intended audience advertisement.

**13. Media Advertising:**

Advertising may be classified on the basis of media. It is called media advertising

**14. Product service advertising:**

It is done as a part of social responsibility by the advertising agency or business organization or government or institution

**15. Financial Advertising:**

It has assumed greater importance in these days. All financial institutions like banks, insurance companies etc take shelter under financial advertising. The copy of financial advertising gives the highlights of the project, details of issues, closing date of issue, profile of the product.

### ACCORDING TO PHILIP KOTLER:

**1. Geographical area:**

(*i*) National

(*ii*) Regional

(*iii*) Local

**2. Content:**

(*i*) Product advertising

(*ii*) Brand advertising

(*iii*) Institutional advertising

**3. Type of appeal:**

(*i*) Factual

(*ii*) Emotional

**4. Audience**

(*i*) Consumer

(*ii*) Industrial

(*iii*) Trade

**5. Sponsor:**

(*i*) Manufacturers

(*ii*) Middlemen

(*iii*) Private

**6. Intended Effort:**

(*i*) Direct Action

(*ii*) Delayed Action

**7. Level of Demand Influence:**

(*i*) Primary product level

(*ii*) Selective brand level

### ACCORDING TO CUNDIFF AND STILL:

**1. On the basis of Geographical area covered:**

(*i*) National

(*ii*) Regional

(*iii*) Local

**2. On the basis of prospects intended to be covered:**

(*i*) Consumer

(*ii*) Industrial

(*iii*) Trade advertising

**3. On the basis of message:**

(*i*) Product

(*ii*) Institutional

**4. On the basis of result intended:**

(*i*) Quick Action

(*ii*) Delayed Action

**5. On the basis of Sponsorship:**

(*i*) Manufacturer

(*ii*) Middlemen or trade group

(*iii*) Industry or retailers

(*iv*) Co-operative advertising.

**6. On the basis of Demand**

(*i*) Primary

(*ii*) Selective

**7. On the basis of Targets defined:**

(*i*) Mass advertising

(*ii*) Class advertising

**8. On the basis of types of appeal:**

(*i*) Rational

(*ii*) Emotional

**ACCORDING TO HARRY L. HANDSON:**

**1. On the basis of Product:**

(*i*) Consumer goods.

(*ii*) Industrial product advertising.

**2. On the basis of persons.**

(*i*) Consumers

(*ii*) Retailers

(*iii*) Whole traders

(*iv*) Manufacturers

**3. On the basis of Media.**

(*i*) News-papers

(*ii*) Magazines

(*iii*) Radio

(*iv*) Television

**4. On the basis of advertising appeals:**

(*i*) Rational

(*ii*) Emotional

**5. On the basis of Business Institutions:**

(*ii*) Retailers

(*iii*) Manufacturers

(*iv*) Wholesalers

**6. On the basis of objective**

(*i*) Creation of demand

(*ii*) Creation of image.

## REVIEW QUESTIONS :

1. What are the general types of Advertising?
2. Write a short note on (*i*) Product Advertising

   (*ii*) Persuasive Advertising

   (*iii*) Institutional Advertising

# 24 BENEFITS/ADVANTAGES/ ROLE OF ADVERTISING

Advertising is an integral part of our economic and social life. It has done wonders in the modern economic world. It has affected every segment of society. It makes distinct contribution to the sales volume, consumers, channels of distribution, manufacturers, sales force, society and community, profitability and overall prosperity which attracts many marketing executives to assign it a relatively more important role in the overall marketing strategy.

It creates a demand for the product and makes it possible for the introduction of mass production, installation of up to date machinery and consequent reduction of the cost of production.

## ADVANTAGES, ROLE, IMPORTANCE, BENEFITS OF ADVERTISING

### I. Manufacturer or Producers:

1. Mass production
2. Increasing the sales
3. Expands to new market
4. Easy introduction of products
5. Reducing the production cost
6. It creates demand
7. It protects the manufacturers against competition
8. It stabilizes the selling price
9. It eliminate the seasonal slumps
10. It creates brand image and goodwill of the manufacturers
11. It helps to establish a direct contact between the manufacturers and the consumer
12. It helps in increasing profits of a company

### II. Business Channels of Distribution: (Middlemen, wholesalers, Retailers)

1. It supplements the selling activities
2. It increases the sales, reduces risk and reduction of overhead expenses
3. The reputation created by advertising is also shared by wholesalers and retailers alike as they are not required to spend anything on advertising and already well advertised product
4. It ensures more economical as selling cost is reduced,
5. It enables them to have production information

6. It facilitates selling because consumers are already aware of the products, its quality, price, durability, uses etc.,
7. It stabilizes the prices and thus avoids losses to wholesalers and retailers through change in the price.

**III. Consumers:**

1. It reduces their shopping time
2. It is useful in taking decisions as to selection of a product.
3. It provides an opportunity to the prospective buyers to compare the merits and demerits of various substitute products.
4. It acts as an informative service and educates the consumers.
5. It helps in eliminating the middlemen
6. It is also responsible for higher standard of living of the consumers.
7. It enhances consumer satisfaction
8. It ensures better quality product at reasonable rate.

**IV. Salesman or Sales force:**

It is the backbone of personnel selling. Thus without advertising salesmanship is incomplete.

1. It prepares necessary colourful background and thus selling efforts are considerably reduced. It makes the task of the salesmanship easier and simpler.
2. It makes introduction of a product quite easy and convenient for the salesman.
3. It supplements the efforts of the sales force. It makes the more effective and productive salesforce.
4. It helps in establishing permanent relationship with the customers.

**V. Community or Society:**

1. Advertisement is creative both directly or indirectly
2. It is responsible for higher standard of living of the people
3. Advertisement in general, is educative in nature
4. It is the advertising revenue that makes the newspapers etc., not only alive but also makes their progress.
5. It also assures employment opportunities to the professional artist.
6. It has been described as the corner stone of culture
7. It promotes art and initiative
8. It is a tool of mass communication

**"Money spent on Advertisement is waste". Do you agree with the statement? Give reasons for your statement?**

In spite of numerous advantages of advertising, various criticisms have been levelled against modern advertising, i.e. it encourages wastefulness, creates monopoly, creates desires that cannot be fulfilled, does not use the media for cultural advantage, takes advantages of emotion, and not reason, increases the cost of goods, ultimately the burden of advertising falls on the poor consumers.

**I. Economic Objection :**

1. It is not productive
2. It increases cost of goods
3. It multiplies the needs of consumers
4. It just takes business from one concern and gives it to another
5. It creates monopoly
6. It encourages waste

**II. Social Objection :**

1. Misrepresentation of facts
2. Wastage of national resources
3. Press is influenced by the advertisers

**III. Ethical objections :**

1. Consumer deficits
2. Birth to social evils
3. Promotes sentimental touch

**IV Legal restrictions :**

Sachaar committee has recommended that the following acts of the sellers should be declared as unfair trade practices and thus be punished accordingly,

1. Misleading advertisements and false representation:
   A seller should not falsely represent,
   (*i*) That the goods are of particular standard, quality, grade, style, composition or model
   (*ii*) That the rebuilt second hand goods are new goods
2. Offering of gifts or prices with the intention of not providing and conducting promotional contest.

## LIMITATIONS OF ADVERTISING

1. Incase the product is not approved by the public then the money spent on advertising process is a waste
2. It is repetitive in nature and it is to be repeated at short intervals. Otherwise its effects will be short lived. Actually reputation is the foundation of modern advertising.
3. If the demand of a product is inelastic then demand cannot be increased by advertising
4. Advertisement done against the basic principles of economy cannot achieve its objectives.

## THE NEED OF ETHICS IN ADVERTISING

1. The advertiser should not make any false statement in his advertising.
2. A model statue should be designed to discourage fraud in advertising
3. Goods should be advertised in such a way that they do not call forth complaints
4. The advertiser should see that this reputation and goodwill is not injured by the advertisement

5. Consumer association should be established in all the ethics which should educate theconsumers not to purchase those products based on false advertisement
6. Civil and criminal liability should be enforced by the Government against false advertising
7. The advertisers should know that the products sold on the basis of false advertisements are short living only. Thus advertising should always be honest.
8. Business man, organizations like chamber of commerce, trade association, business bureau etc should discourage unfair commercial practices; Actions should be taken against persons making false advertising.
9. There must be censor ship of advertising both by public and private sector.

## DISTINCTION BETWEEN ADVERTISING AND PUBLICITY

According to Definition Committee of the American Marketing Association," *Publicity can be defined as any form commercially significant news about a product, an institution, a service or a person published in space or Radio time that is not paid for by the sponsor."*

Advertising and publicity, the aim of both are same and they carry the same message. However they slightly differ in nature and may be distinguished as under:

- Advertising is paid by the sponsor and hence it is commercial transaction. On the other hand publicity is not paid by the sponsor and thus it does not have commercial features.
- Advertising is always non-personal whereas the publicity may be both personal and non-personal.
- The object of advertising is to attract the customers and induce them to make purchases. The object of publicity is to make use of the enterprise, irrespective of the fact whether the public is influenced or not by the publicity.
- The expenses of advertisement are paid by the advertiser, where as the publicity's free
- The scope of advertisement is limited as compared to publicity.
- The advertisement bears the name of the advertiser whereas the publicity does not.

## REVIEW QUESTIONS:

1. Discuss the importance of advertising.
2. "Money spent on advertisement is wasteful" – Do you agree?
3. Discuss the need for ethics in Advertisement.
4. Distinguish between advertisement and publicity.
5. What are the limitations of advertising?

# 25 AIDAS

The effectiveness of advertising depends upon to what extent the advertising message is received and accepted by the targeted audience. Advertising is to be effective from the following activities.

- Attract attention
- Secure Interest
- Build desire for the product and obtain action

The most important and popular slogan of advertisement is AIDAS. The expansion of *AIDAS* is

A – Attention

I – Interest

D – Desire

A – Action

S – Satisfaction

### ATTENTION

The layout is the most important factor that directs the attention of the target through an advertisement. The size of advertisement also computes as to get attracted to it. Movement is also an important element for getting attention. It may be physical or emotional. Position, Size, Colour, Movement, Language, Model, Selection, Placement, Timing, Illustration etc., are such factors which contribute to attention.

### INTEREST

Advertisement seen does not mean advertisement read. As a matter of fact mostly people see the illustration and do not read the copy as they feel it burden job. The advertisement should have suitable headlines. The selection of the illustration and its integration to live are very important.

### DESIRE

The basic objective of advertising is to create a desire for the product or service being advertised. Appeals are used for the motivation of people. Buying motivates, physiological as well as psychological, make people to purchase a particular product. The advertiser has to convince the audience by giving evidence by testimonial, endorsement, facts and figures so as to win their faith.

### ACTION

In case the advertisement is successful in attracting the attention, developing interest and creating a desire for the product in the minds of the prospect then the last and most important stage is the action of the prospect. It is the final stage and thus is also called behavior stage. The success of this stage is success of advertisement too. The action may be direct or indirect. In the case of direct action the prospect may immediately place the order of the product. In the case of indirect action, the action can be done at the time of purchase.

## SATISFACTION

After convincing and purchasing of the product by the prospect, suddenly they consume and they can satisfy about the product.

## ADVERTISIBILITY

Every product cannot be advertised. A product must possess certain characteristics to be able to advertise. The ability of a product to be advertised is called advertisibility. A product to have advertisability should possess the following main characteristics.

### 1. Creation of demand (or) Demand Expandability:

The product must be such demand may be created by means of advertising. The demand is expandable, if there is increase in sales due to advertising without any change in prices.

### 2. Hidden Qualities of the product:

Hidden qualities offer better opportunities for advertising

### 3. Differential of a product:

The degree to which the product of a particular brand differs from competing brand is a factor of special significance in determining its advertisibility

### 4. Emotional buying motives:

A product which possesses emotional buying motive can be advertised more effectively to create demand by appealing to such motives.

### 5. Creation of wide market:

They create a wide market for the sale of the products; which is due to the advertisibility of the product concerned.

### 6. Nature of the product:

Advertisibility of a product also depends upon the nature of the product as well as the type of demand in the market

## REVIEW QUESTIONS:

1. Expand and explain the term "AIDAS"
2. What is Advertisibility?
3. What are the characteristics of Advertisibility?

# 26 ADVERTISING PLANNING

It is managerial responsibility of giving advertising plan. An advertising plan is a statement about advertising for a particular product or a service or an institution for the future. The plan states the goods and describes in detail the nature of advertising program of a company. Advertising plan fall with in the corporate plan, because advertising is a specific activity of marketing efforts which is only an integral part of total activities of business.

**A successful advertising plan touches as five ingredients namely:**

1. The goal of the advertiser.
2. The strategies to accomplish the goals.
3. Specific tactics that will be followed in carrying out the creative and media strategies of the advertiser.
4. Description of the kinds of taste.
5. Description of advertising research.

An effective advertising planning helps to know and answer the following relevant questions.

**1. How much to spend on advertising?**

The exact amount to be spent is dependent on a number of variables and is indicated by the advertising budget. The factors accountable are the objectives to be obtained the extent of coverage involved, the extent of competition size and the experience of the firm.

**2. When and how frequently to advertise?**

It is a continuous activity. A sound advertising planning sets an optimum continuity level.

**3. What alternative media to employ?**

For instance some media appeal to eyes, some to eyes and ears and some eyes, ears and brain. An advertising plan should consider this significant issue of media planning and selection of media.

**4. What an advertisement says?**

What a given advertisement says – stands for the advertising creative strategy. Advertising creative strategy states what advertising will communicate about the product, service or institution and specifies the relation of advertising message to consumer needs, wants, desire and dreams. Thus creative planning of advertisement covers the activities of idea development and translation of the same into a final sales message to be directed to the expected audience.

**5. What advertising is attaining?**

The areas of advertising evaluation are – markets – motives – messages – media and the overall results. Thus the advertisements can be most effective in reaching the objectives for which they have been designed.

## STEPS IN ADVERTISING PLANNING PROCESS

### 1. Study of micro and macro environment:

The external environmental factors that is surrounded by the organization is called macro factors which are external to the firm such as social, economical, ethical, political, physical and technological. This factor consists of forces like consumers, competition and price. The micro environmental factors are those which are internal to the organization. These related to the corporate history, psychology, culture, opportunities, threats, etc.

### 2. Setting of organizational goals:

There can't be any organization with out the goals. These goals are broad guidelines that pave the way for reaching the final destination. These may be consumer satisfaction, profit maximization, community service, and social development and so on that lead finally to quality of life.

### 3. Defining the target market:

Market stands for people with purchasing power and willing to accept the product or services or ideas. The company is to move from market potential to sales potential and finally sales forecast. Here target market is one which the company wants to concentrate. Markets are based on many variables such as income, geographical area, level of education, benefits, usages, loyalty, occasion and so on.

### 4. Conducting market research:

It stands for the methods of finding and analyzing facts to assist managers, to make rational decisions. Its scope is vast and covers all the four 'Ps' of marketing mix, namely Price, Product, Promotion, Physical distribution. In addition it covers motivation, advertising policy, sales research which are closely inter related.

### 5. Defining marketing objectives:

Among the basic marketing goals, the worth objectives are survival, growth, innovation, productivity, profit, increased market share, increased sales, reduced cost, quality of service leading to consumer satisfaction and meeting social obligation.

### 6. Designing a Marketing plan:

A marketing plan is the instrument to implement the marketing concept. It is one which links the firms and the markets. It is the foundation for all corporate planning. It is the document of future course of action that spells out as to how the resources at the command of the firm are to be deployed to attain the marketing goals.

### 7. Determining the marketing strategy:

The firm must have a set of policies and strategies. A policy is a broad guideline for thinking and action. Strategy is the counter plan to face market pressures. It is a comprehensive plan of action designed to meet the need of a certain enterprise operating in particular environment.

### 8. Determining Advertising goals:

The general goal of advertising is to increase the sales and profits of the firm and satisfy the user. The common goals are supporting personal selling efforts, reaching people beyond the sales, improving dealers' relationship, increasing market shares, improving the reputation, survival, diversification and so on.

**9. Preparation of Advertising Budgets:**

A successful advertising management is a matter of financial discipline and expertise. Any advertising plan covers the areas of media selection etc. Once media selection is done, its preparation or designing takes place ie. Designing of an advertisement copy made up of copy headline, sub headlines, the text, illustration, slogan and logo, including border line and so on, in print media.

**10. Testing the advertisement plan:**

The advertising plan which has the approval and financial sanction; is to be implemented as to its content in terms of amount, time, and media mix and so on. Implementation is to see that everything is going according to a chartered plan. Planning of advertisement activity is really creative.

**11. Executing the advertising plan:**

The advertising plan setting appropriate goals, planning the operation and putting the plan in to action and monitoring the implementation which setting are continuous one. An advertising budget is a plan that sets the limits on the advertising expenditure, states how expenses will be allocated and controls the disbursement of funds over a period of time, normally one year.

**12. Evaluating the Advertising plan:**

The managerial responsibility in the area of advertising does not come to an end with the execution of an advertising program. Evaluation of advertising effectiveness refers to the managerial exercise aimed at relating the advertising results established. Standards of performance and objectives have access to the real value of advertising performance. This evaluation exercise is also known as advertising research.

## REVIEW QUESTIONS:

1. Why the advertisers prepare the planning?
2. What are the ingredients of Advertising planning?
3. What are the steps followed in advertising planning process?

# 27 ADVERTISING BUDGET

## HOW MUCH TO SPEND?

Advertising expenditure Decisions are often arbitrary and at times merely a guess. In many Companies, advertising is an extremely vital force in the success of their marketing endeavors. Not only by business, but even by the government and social welfare organizations, the useful role of advertising has been recognized. Advertising is a Powerful marketing tool; but it is highly expensive too. Companies Spend huge Sums of money on advertising alone.

## WHAT IS BUDGET?

A budget is a financial quantitative statement prepared prior to a definite period of time, of the policy to be pursued during that period for the purpose of achieveing a given objective. The budget is prepared by taking various factors of income and expenditure.

### Thus a Budget:

(*i*) Is a formal statement of estimated income and expenditure for a fixed period, generally a year.

(*ii*) Is a statement of policies to be followed by the Concern or department during the budget period.

(*iii*) Is prepared in advance. The budget figures, there fore, are only estimates.

What is advertising Budget?

It is a functional budget setting the goals and objectives in terms of income and expenditure on advertising during a specified period. It translates advertising plan into money. It includes sales goals, product facts, marketing information, Competitive situation, creative platforms and rough examples of treatment. It sets forth and analyses marketing and advertising strategies copy and media recommendations for that strategy and plans and schedules. The budget may specify....

(i) Financial Capabilities of the Company and

(*ii*) Allocation of funds into various specific operations.

## STEPS IN 'ADVERTISING BUDGET' MAKING PROCESS

Actual budgetary process consists of four major Steps:

1. Collection of data and preparation of budget.
2. Presentation and approval of the budget.
3. Budget execution and
4. Control of Budget or Budgetary Control.

### (1) Collection of data and preparation of budget

Agency personnel are responsible for the planning of advertising work. The planning of advertising work is subjected to various information which the research people provide to the department or agency personnel. On the basis of such information, the men concerned get insight for decisions dealing with target markets, products, packaging, advertising copy, new product introductions and media selection. Having decided upon on the above variables, the person concerned takes a decision on the very important issue "how much to spend for advertising".

Determining the size of the future advertising appropriation is the first step in preparing the advertising budget. Once this figure has been set through any of the various methods the total advertising budget should, then, be allocated among various media and advertising functions.

In other words, the whole bread should be cut into slices. The budget must be allocated among different market segments, time periods and geographical areas depending upon the market potential within that segment, period or area.

### (2) Presentation and approval of the budget

The next step in the budget making process, after it is developed by the advertising head in consultation with the agency personnel is to present it before the chief executive officer of the company or vice president or manager of marketing department for approval. Chief executive of the firm or the marketing manager before assigning his approval on the budget may consult the firm's chief executive or financial committee and heads of the other concerned or related departments. Chief executive and financial committee act as a watchdog over company's total fund and involve themselves in allocating the available funds to the various activities according to their importance in the organization keeping in view the organizational goals in order to maximize overall profits. These executives may adjust the budget specifications on the basis of appropriations or refer it to the advertising manager to review it accordingly.

### (3) Budget Execution

Administration of advertising spending is some what a routine activity. The prime task undertaken for this purpose is the purchase of authorized time and space over the media and the agency handles the job for and on behalf of advertiser.

The costs of advertising production such as making television channels, can also be significant elements in the over all expenditure for advertising. These are also incurred by the agency on behalf of the client. The advertising manager should be certain that the expenses are made in accordance with the approved plan and in economical manner.

### (4) Control of Budget

It is the duty of the advertising manager to see whether actual advertising expenditure coincide with the budgeted expenditure or not. A procedure must be evolved which bring information about current expenditure to the attention of the advertising manager. The figure of actual expenditure should then be compared with the planned expenditure. Both must run parallel if the budget is to serve as a control.

## ADVERTISING BUDGET METHODS OF APPROPRIATION

An Advertising budget is referred to as an organized plan made out for expenditure of money on advertisement. It translates plan into action. The advertising man while developing advertising budget has to consider several factors before giving it a final shape, appropriating the amount to be spent on advertisement. Such variable are population and income trend, economic situation, competitive behavior, product improvement and sales force etc.

Cost factor is one of the deciding factors in determining the size of the budget. A cost analysis study of different media of advertisement and their effectiveness should be considered while preparing the budget.

## METHODS OF APPROPRIATION

Simply stated every manufacturer sets apart a sum of money to be spending on advertising which is referred to as advertising appropriation.

The amount is not fixed arbitrarily but is determined on some scientific basis.

The following methods are more commonly used in determining the size of the advertising budget or in making appropriation for advertising.

1. Availability of funds
2. Percentage of sales method
3. Return on investment method
4. Competitive parity approach
5. Objective and task approach
6. Judgment method

### 1. Availability of funds approach

This approach considers the total funds available with the Company. Out of the total funds the company has to decide how much it can afford for advertising. For this purpose company forecast its anticipated sales and margins.

In this approach, it has been assumed that advertising is a residual activity that is funded only after resources have been allocated to other corporate function, which are presumably deemed to be more important. Thus advertising activity is ranked last. It is possible that the allocation is too small to allow advertising to be very effective.

The basic weakness of this approach is that it does not answer "how much should we spend on advertising". Thus one producer may price his products high enough to yield the revenue necessary for sufficient advertising impact. One of his competitors, on the other hard, uses all the receipts above a minimum amount to advertise new products, In effect, the second company is borrowing from profits and other resources to push its new products during their growth phase.

### 2. Percentage on sales method

Under this method, the amount to be appropriated to advertising is arrived at by multiplying the value of past year's sales or the projected sales for the budget period with a pre-determined percentage. Different percentages may be fixed for different products, territories, market targets or other break–downs depending upon the way in which sales forecasts have been broken down.

### 3. Return on investment method

In this method, advertising expenditure is considered as an investment rather than expenditure. This approach is no doubt correct as the returns one gets from advertising are generally spread over a period of time. In effect, the advertising expenditure in one year generates sales for years and therefore returns on this investment inflows for years. The advertising budget is prepared; under this method by taking into account the increased profits generated by an increase in sales and goodwill through the advertising.

**4. Competitive parity approach**

Another traditional approach for appropriating the amount for advertising expenditure is to consider the amount spent by the competitive firms in the same industry on advertising either on an absolute or a relative basis. This approach quite ignores its own promotional objective and considers what its competitors are spending on advertising.

This approach is based on the assumption that competitors have similar problems and strategies. It is common to monitor the marketing program of competitors. As a part of this activity, firms assess the advertising efforts of major competitors and the industry as a whole.

**5. Objective and task approach**

Probably, the objective and task approach of setting the advertising budget is the most desirable approach. This method is goal oriented. Under this method marketing objectives are fixed after intensive market research. The advertising cost of each relevant task such as type of media, frequency of advertising, etc are then calculated. The aggregate cost of this entire task may be assumed to be the firm's advertising budget.

## ADVERTISING BUDGET MODELS

### Statistical Advertising Budget Models

One modeling approach concentrates on determining an optimal total advertising budget without specifically considering creative design or media decisions. This model is based on developing a functional relationship between advertising expenditure and some measure of desired market response, usually sales. Data are collected on both sales and advertising expenditure for some previous time period in order to estimate the relationship between the two models usually of the form

$$S = a + b_1 X_1 + b_2 x_2 + \dots\dots\dots\dots b_n x_n + U$$

Where $S$ = sales of a product brand

$X_1$ = advertising expenditure

$X_2$ - $Xn$ = other variables thought to influence sales, such as competitors advertising, disposable personal income, etc.,

$b_1$ - $b_n$ = Parameters estimated from the data showing the relationship of the corresponding variables to sales.

$U$ = random error.

If the analysis of data shows that a model sufficient explains sales variations and that advertising is significantly related to sales, it may aid in the budgeting decisions, by plugging in the sales objective for the brand being advertised and estimates for each of the $X_2$ to $X_n$ variables. The size of the advertising budget required to achieve the sales goal can be computed.

More recent work on statistical advertising sales models has increased their complexity and descriptiveness by considering several factors, which control the budget decision.

First, econometric techniques have been used to incorporate the cumulative effects of advertising on sales. This recognizes that current sales are dependent on current advertising and a carry over effect from previous period advertising. In addition, the inter relationships between the advertising budget and creative decisions may be assessed by including the variables representing the copy design.

The data for statistical advertising budget models may be generated in several different ways. Time series data may be used when a firm has kept records of sales, advertising expenditures and other variables included in the model over enough past periods to provide a sufficient number of data points.

## REVIEW QUESTIONS:

1. What is advertising budget?
2. Discuss the steps involved in advertisement budget making process.
3. Discuss various methods of advertisement budget appropriation.

# 28 ADVERTISING DECISIONS

The important point is that advertising decisions are influenced by their interaction with marketing objectives. Advertising does not exist in isolation, but must deal with and reinforce the rest of the marketing program. In fact all components of the marketing mix should strike a balance with each other. They should be in consonance with each other and should contribute to the organizations marketing objectives in their totality. For instance, advertising objectives should be derived from the marketing objective as a whole and there should be no conflict between them.

### Factors Influencing the Marketing Mix

Factors which tend to influence the marketing mix are :

a. The marketing objectives.

b. The attitudes and behavior patterns of potential consumers.

c. Attitudes and motivation of the trade

d. Characteristics of the products or the service to be sold.

e. Competitor's strategies.

All decisions taken at the planning stage will affect the communication strategy and the advertising program should reflect the type of results advertising should produce out of several alternatives such as the following:

a. Increased brand awareness

b. Improved brand opinion

c. Change in the market share

d. An attitudinal change

e. Motivation of actual purchase

f. Short term gains in profits and for sales

g. Medium -long term gains in contribution, profits and sales.

The function of advertising is to create awareness amongst the target audience, to ensure correct comprehension of the message and move the prospects close to conviction, and finally to buying action. Advertising effort may sometimes be designed to have an effect on all levels at the same time. To begin with let us assume that the market is equally divided into the following five levels.

| | | |
|---|---|---|
| Action | : | 20% are present users of the product (action) |
| Conviction | : | 20% are convinced but have not go he around to buying. |

| | | |
|---|---|---|
| Comprehension | : | 20% comprehend the product, but are not convinced. |
| Awareness | : | 20% are aware of the production but not of its advantages. |
| Un- awareness | : | 20% never heard of it. |

The objectives of the advertising campaign may then be defined as "moving 10% of the target audience from the unawareness to the awareness stage and further in the above hierarchy to eventually achieve 10%increase in sales". In their case, advertising has worked "across the board" i.e. it has moved people from "unawareness to awareness, others from comprehension to conviction and action:

## REVIEW QUESTIONS:

1. State the factors influencing marketing mix.

# 29 ADVERTISING STRATEGY

Strategy provides the link between advertising objectives and plans, and paves the ground for their implementation. It can be instrumental in prioritizing various objectives, taking into account the attitudinal framework as well as corporate and marketing goals, and the market situation and characteristics.

Boyd, Ray and Strong suggest the following five broad strategy alternatives for influencing attitudinal structures.

(*i*) Affect those forces, which influence strongly the choice criteria for evaluating brands belonging to the product class.

(*ii*) Add characteristics to those considered salient to the product class.

(*iii*) Increase / decrease the rating for salient product class characteristics.

(*iv*) Change the perception of the company's brand with regard to some particular salient product characteristics.

(*v*) Change the perception of a competitive brand with regard to some particular salient product characteristics.

In the marketing framework, advertising strategy will be based on considerations such as the following.

(i) Company's standing and its strength and weaknesses.

(ii) Product history and its life cycle stage

(iii) Positioning of the product as indicated by perceptual mapping.

(iv) Existing and anticipated competition.

(v) Support needed by sales force and distribution channels

(vi) Appropriation for advertising against the background of the company's financial planning and constraints.

(vii) Availability of media to cover the target audience.

(viii) The total promotional package including sales promotion at the dealer and consumer level.

It must be remembered that both attitudinal and marketing contexts are relevant for developing advertising strategy. This systematic approach helps in resolving any contradictions.

## REVIEW QUESTIONS:

1. What is advertising strategy?
2. Discuss the alternative strategies for institutional attitudinal structures.

# 30 ORGANIZING ADVERTISING CAMPAIGN

## WHAT IS CAMPAIGN PLANNING?

The word campaign in advertising management is used in the sense of organized and careful planned use of paid publicity for the accomplishment of a definite purpose, planning is a management term and connects the decision making aspect of future activities in present. It is deciding what to do in future. It determines the goals and the various steps in achieving those goals. Thus campaign planning means deciding in advance what is to be done and how the allocated advertising campaign are to be utilized in the best manner, towards achieving the marketing purpose. Various information and parameters are considered for campaign planning.

## MAJOR PARAMETERS

The major parameters under which the campaign consultants operate are:

(i) The Socio economic-cum-demographic profile of the customers

(ii) The total advertising appropriation.

(iii) Media availability: Space or time on the media.

(iv) The client and the product or service profile.

(v) The Campaign period: Short term or long term

(vi) The timing of the campaign: day or night or once, twice, or thrice a day.

(vii) Marketing advertising objectives.

(viii) The distribution set-up through agencies or whole sales or direct supply to retailers or direct sale to consumers through multiple chain system.

(ix) The competitor's activities - type design and appeal of advertising used by competitors and media used by them.

(x) The special group in the marketing environment.

(xi) A review of past advertising – make a change in the campaign planning.

(xii) The creative requirements taking consumers, attitude and market behavior into consideration.

(xiii) The new plans.

## THE OBJECTIVES OF AN ADVERTISING CAMPAIGN PLANNING

(a) To determine the market for the product: size of the market, target consumers, purchase authority in the family, the time of purchase.

(b) To decide the channels of Distribution.

(c) To determine the scope of the campaign.

(d) To determine the media.

(e) To discover the central idea.

(f) To determine the time, Date and time of appearance.

(g) To prepare advertising copy.

(h) To prepare and use the budget.

(i) To determine tone of advertising, fundamental human desire, media and the amount of space or time and co-operation.

## PRINCIPLES OF CAMPAIGN PLANNING

The basic principles of campaign planning which should be emphasized are:

**(1) Definition:** The main principle of campaign planning is to define the campaign objective into clear focus so that efforts may be made in the direction.

**(2) Concentration:** The planners must avoid dispersal of resources over too many different objectives or media. Emphasis should be concentrated to some extent, only to a few objectives or media.

**(3) Domination:** The one important factor in campaign planning should be to ensure that the campaign dominates its competitors in some part of the market at some points and takes control of the mind and interest of the potential customers.

**(4) Repetition:** Repetition is a must to provide for the continuation of the message regularly just to remind the attributes of the product.

## PLANNING OF AN ADVERTISING CAMPAIGN

The marketing programme of most business firms contains a basic element of advertising. It is the best method of communication with the marketing organizations and it is the prime responsibility of the management to plan, organize and control the advertising programmes. Advertising campaign is one of the important parts of the advertising programmes. Underlying an effective advertising programme therefore, is a sound marketing planning that stabilizes the inter relationship of all elements in the marketing mix. Basic marketing plans may remain effective for a period of years and provide a foundation for many advertising programmers and a number of advertising campaigns.

## BASIC STEPS IN CAMPAIGN PROGRAMME

In planning an advertising campaign, the advertiser has taken seven essential steps.

### 1. Appraisal of Advertising Opportunity

This is the first step in planning the campaign. Before an advertising campaign is planned, the advertiser must determine whether the advertiser has a role to play in a particular marketing situation. The study of the economic effects of advertising postulates five conditions to govern the opportunity for advertising. These five conditions are:

(*i*) Presence of a favourable primary demand.

(*ii*) Good Chance for product differentiation

  (*i*) There must be hidden qualities.

  (*ii*) Powerful emotional buying motives.

  (*iii*) Adequacy of funds.

**2. Analyzing the market:**

Analysis of market, answers two important questions

(i) Where are we now?

(ii) Why are we there?

In this process, the most critical decision is to define closely the target market for the product. One of the target market are consumers known as advertising campaign and to suit those people it may be designed.

The advertisers over all marketing plan provides the basis for a current analysis of target market and a projection of current market conditions. When the campaign actually appears various factors are to be considered for the planning.

**External Factors:** Total industry volume of sales (total demand) over a period of time, the advertisers share in the total turn over for the industry, competitors share in the industry turn over, the legal constraint placed on the product category and the role of foreign competition are some external factors.

**Internal Factors:** Firm's financial and production capabilities. Both types of factors are essential for planning and advertising campaign.

**3. Determining Advertising Objectives**

In the absence of objectives nothing can be planned. So planning of any business activity starts with he setting of objectives by the top management. Marketing objectives are also set in pursuance of the over all business objectives and advertising objectives are determined in pursuance of marketing objectives. The different advertising objectives should be carefully ranked by their relative importance.

The statement of objectives for a new advertising campaign should contain four elements:

(i) The basic message to be delivered

(ii) The audience.

(iii) The intended effect.

(iv) The specific criteria to measure the success of the campaign later.

**4. Establishing the Budget and Necessary Control Systems**

Once the advertising objectives are determined the funds necessary to achieve the objectives must be provided for. A large sum is being spent on-advertising in the modern business it is important to budget the amount carefully to be sure that they are spent widely.

Advertising budget is a plan for financing certain future advertising operations with in a specified period of time, usually a year. It should be constantly reviewed in terms of changing marketing situations.

Deciding how much to spend on advertising is the most perplexing problem. It is very difficult to measure its effectiveness in terms of profits or sales volume.

**5. Developing the Strategy**

Having laid down the objectives of advertising, an appropriate strategy is to be developed to achieve those objectives. Advertising strategy is creativity applied to knowledge for the purpose of finding the most effective way of achieving an end.

Strategy issue arises in two major area of advertising.

(i) Selecting Advertising media.

(ii) Creating Advertising messages.

**6. Coordinating Advertising with other Promotional methods**

Advertising, to be fully effective, needs active support from the channels of distribution and other sub advertising components of the marketing organizations. In this area, co-operation must be sought from distributors, dealers and sales people. The effort to get this co-operation is known as merchandising and advertising. It makes the job of dealers and sales people easier. There are various ways in which advertising is merchandised to the sales force and to dealers.

**7. Evaluating Advertising Results**

As soon as the campaign is underway it can be subjected to testing within a stimulated marketing environment. There may be two types of testing.

(i) Pre–testing and

(ii) Post–testing

**Pre–testing:**

Pre – testing is done before and may influence the buying media and the creative steps yet to come. It is a research technique to know the reactions to the advertising by a representative sample of the target market before the advertiser spends a sizeable amount on campaign.

**Post-testing**

It is done only after the full commitment to a creative approach and a schedule of media has been made. The main objectives of post testing are to learn the weaknesses and successes of the existing campaign and use such knowledge in planning the future campaigns more effective.

**Responsibility for execution**

Planning the advertising Programme is the prime responsibility of the advertiser who delegates some of the task to the advertising agency. Execution of plan on the other hand is, usually, performed by the advertising agency and the advertiser reviews and controls the plan. Execution of one phase is frequently in progress while planning for another programme.

## REVIEW QUESTIONS:

1. What is campaign planning?
2. What are the major parameters of advertising campaign?
3. Discuss the objectives of an advertising campaign planning.
4. What are the principles of campaign planning?
5. What are the basic steps in campaign planning?
6. Write a short note on i. Pre-testing ii. Post testing

# 31 CREATIVITY OF ADVERTISEMENT COPY

## WHAT IS CREATIVITY?

Creative part of advertising involves the process of selecting and presenting the advertising message. It may also be known as the art of advertising. The business of conceiving the ideas, writing of message, designing and producing the advertisement copies is called Advertising creativity. The success of advertising depends upon the quality of the message or copy of advertisement. Creativity is an art. Artists, associated with this art combine the product attributes with the ideas, words and phrases to persuade the consumer to buy the product. A major part of advertising budget is spent on this creative part. Creativity task is to determine what to say and how to say.

## ACTIVITY COMPRISING CREATIVE DESIGN TASK PROCESS

The following activities are parts of creative design Process:

(1) Advertising Communications objectives.

(2) Collecting information about the product and marketing mix.

(3) Demographic and Psychographics break – up of the specific target audience.

(4) A thought for designing the layout and advertising copy.

(5) Credibility or back – up claims supported by facts.

(6) Copy layout tests before finalization.

(7) Allocation of funds to creative task.

(8) Creating Strategy and tactics.

## QUALITIES OF A GOOD ADVERTISEMENT COPY

The importance of a good advertisement copy can hardly be overemphasized. All the planning research and expense would go waste if proper care is not taken in drafting an advertisement copy that will achieve the purpose of advertising. The psychological aims of an advertisement are that the public must be made to:

(i) Look,

(ii) Like,

(iii) Learn and

(iv) Buy

In other words a scientifically drafted copy should:

(a) Attract primary initial attention

(b) Hold attention in an interesting way, awaken and stimulate interest.

(c) Bring about an association of an impression, which will have permanence or memory value.

(d) Convince persuade, and induce to purchase the product

(e) Suggest and lead to specific response to encourage the decision to buy.

The aim of advertising copy is that it shall be seen, read the message conveyed and then act upon. An advertisement copy which fails in attracting the attention of the prospects and create an urge in their minds for possessing the product will naturally be of no use though a large sum has been spent on advertising the product by the advertiser. An expert has set down some 'musts' of a good advertising copy.

(i) It must make people see it.

(ii) It must make people read it.

(iii) It must make people understand it.

(iv) It must make people believe it.

(v) It must make people want your product.

A good copy of advertisement should possess following characteristics or qualities or values:

1. Attention value.
2. Suggestive value.
3. Memorizing value.
4. Conviction value.
5. Sentimental value.
6. Education value.
7. Instinctive value.

**1. Attention value:**

An advertising copy must attract the attention of the potential consumers. It should be designed in such a fashion that the attention of a busiest person may be drawn immediately. Various devices can be used to make the copy attractive such as use of pictures, use of display, type or heading, border, price quotation, reply coupons

**2. Suggestive value:**

Having attracted the attention of the reader the next task would be to offer a suggestion about the use and the utility of the product that may remain inscribed on the mind of the reader even when he forget where he really saw the advertisement, slogans, pictures, phrases and suggestions may be used for this purpose.

**3. Memorizing value:**

The copy of the advertisement should be so drafted and laid out that the product will stick to the mind of the individual reader. Repetition of advertisement, with slogan is an effective method of creating a memorizing value.

**4. Conviction value:**

Advertising can prove effective and achieve the desired end when the suggestion contained in it is backed by convincing arguments.

*Ex: "STOP BAD BREATH WITH COLGATE WHILE YOU FIGHT TOOTH DECAY ALL DAY "*

**5. Sentimental value:**

Sentimental value plays a very important role in advertising, particularly in the case of food articles. Sentiments reflect the personal feeling and attitude of an individual. They indicate reactions of a person in favour or against a particular product.

For example ***"Be Indian buy Indian"*** appeal is directed towards national sentiments of the people.

Advertiser should prepare separate copy for different market keeping in view the sentiments and likes and dislikes.

**6. Educational value:**

A good copy of advertisement must possess educative value because the object of modern advertising is not merely to satisfy the existing demand but to create future demand. So a good copy of advertisement should educate the general public about the uses of the new product or the new uses of the same product.

e.g.: Advertisement issued by Hindustan lever ltd., suggests new methods for preparing Palatable food with vanaspathy..

**7. Instrinctive Appeal value:**

Human thoughts and actions are guided by instincts. All that one thinks or does has its roots in one instinct or the other. Instincts are the underlying forces which compel the men to act in certain ways. The most important function of an advertisement copy is to induce, persuade and motivate the prospects to think well of a product and to take it to use.

Generally speaking the following are the basic instincts which an advertiser should keep in his mind.

**(a) Self – preservation Instinct :**

The sale of products like medicines cloths etc, may be promoted by appeal to this anxiety.

**(b) Hoarding Instinct:**

Banking institutions, insurance companies or other government and non-government saving organizations serve to hoarding instinct of the people. Slogans like 'UP AND UP GO YOUR SAVINGS' may be used for this purpose.

**(c) Parental Instinct:**

Parental instinct takes the form of love and affection for the children. Those advertisers who deal in children's requirements like garments, toys, baby food etc may promote this instinct in parents.

**(d) Self Display Instinct:**

Instinct of self display is promoted by the advertiser of ready made clothing, women's dresses, jewellery etc.,

**(e) Something for Nothing Instinct:**

This instinct is widely used by lottery ticket sellers by offering one free ticket with the purchase of 10 tickets or by drycleaners by the offering three for two bargains.

On the basic of the above basic instincts, the following themes or central ideas may be laid down for advertisement copies meant to advertise different types of products :Pride

1. Economy
2. Parental Attention
3. Beauty
4. Comfort

5. Patriotism
6. Limitation
7. Health
8. Fear
9. Achievement

Thus a good advertisement copy must possess the above qualities to make it an ideal advertisement.

## CLASSIFICATION OF ADVERTISING COPY

It is true that copy writing is an art and the copy writer has a very important role to play in advertising creativity. Copywriting does not admit any stereotyped rules and classification. There are various styles in which a copy can be prepared and presented. The following types of copy may be studied.

**1. Descriptive copy:**

This type of copy describes the pertinent and relevant features of the product. It is very simple and non-technical in nature.

**2. Scientific copy:**

Such types of copies are technical in nature and generally used by drugs and pharmaceutical firms elaborating the propositions of properties and constituents of the product. It provides full information about the product and the producer.

**3. Institutional copy:**

It aims at selling the name of the advertiser or the institution that is producing or selling the products or services. The main objective of such type of advertisement is to create maintain or increase the good-will of the product or of brand or of the department or of the selling house as a whole.

**4. Topical copy:**

It commands a good deal of interest because of that sensational event which lives in minds of the public.

**5. Human Interest copy:**

It makes its appeal to the emotions and the senses rather than to the intellect and judgment. Sympathy, fear, bonus, curiosity and other emotional appeals like appeals to the senses of slight hearing, touch, taste, and smell are used in such type of copy.

Human interest copy can take various forms:-

Humorous copy, Fear Copy, Story copy, Predicament copy

**7. Conversational copy:**

The Conversational copy presents the message in the way of conversation. It uses an informal language and conversation takes place in terms of 'I' and 'you' with personal reference to reader and the advertiser.

**8. Personality copy:**

This copy attempts to the opinion of personality real or imaginary – about the product. Usually the personality is real.

**9. Prestige copy:**

This pattern is usually for an institutional advertising, which aims at creating an atmosphere about the product or the firm and may not directly advertise the product for sale.

**10. Educational copy:**

The copy is designed to educate the general public about the attributes of the product. Usually introductory appeal is made in this style when the product is introduced in the market for the first time; it is the duty of every producer or advertiser to tell everything relevant about the product to the public in such a manner, that it may get a warm welcome among customers.

**11. Suggestive copy:**

A Suggestive copy tries to suggest or convey the message to the readers directly or indirectly to persuade them to purchase the product.

**12. Questioning copy:**

Questioning copy as the term suggests incorporates a series of questions expected to be answered by the readers.

For example:

Do you want luxuriant hair?

Do you want a sound sleep?

Do you want clear eyesight?

## COMPONENTS OF AN ADVERTISING COPY

An advertising copy is the means by which the advertiser's ideas are given expression to in a message to readers. Regardless of its length and brevity, copy refers to all the reading matters of an advertisement, including the headline, sub – headings, text or body and the name of the firm or the standard initials of the advertiser.

The first copy conforms to the requisites of a good copy. A copy writer must take pains in making up a sound advertisement copy containing its various components (ie) headlines, sub – headings, illustrations etc.,

The following are the main components of an advertisement copy

1. Headline 2. Subheadings 3. Slogans 4. Illustrations 5. Text or body of the copy 6. Identification marks

**1. Headline:** The first device in a copy is headline. Its main purpose is to attract attention, arouse curiosity or interest and there by induce further reading. It should be as short as possible and pleasantly warded to any of the instincts.

**Types of Headlines**

**(a) Label Headlines :**

A label heading identifies the name of the products

e.g. LIMCA, THUMSUP – The Refreshing Cola.

**(b) Informative Headlines:**

Information headlines give information about the product.

"Super Surf Washes" whiter

**(c) Provocate Headline:**

Such type of headlines is generally used when an article is introduced in the market for the first time.

Eg: Stomach Trouble? Only two RENNIE tablets are sufficient.

**(d) Selective Headlines:**

It seeks climate by directing appeal to those for whom the product holds interest. It eliminates all other readers, for whom the product is not appealing.

E.g.: Attention – Importers

Car owners! Save one-liter petrol in every ten liter

**(e) Direct Command Headline:**

Direct Command headline asks the reader to buy the particular article.

E.g.: Don't say ink – Say BRIL

**(f) Question Headline:**

Such headlines put questions to the reader and suggest the solution in using the particular article.

E.g.: Are you short of hearing? Use ARPHI

**2. Sub-headlines :**

These are subordinate captions that simply expand the headline thoughts. They carry the readers interest a step further.

For example, the headline in an advertisement for Unit Trust of India – Listen to ours highs and our laws a sub-headline then explained that, "An all time high a 14.25% dividend. An exciting low just Rs12.75 per unit.

Thus Sub headlines Serve the following three purposes

1. They gain attention and interest of the readers
2. They organize the copy into logically related segments and thus ease the reading task and
3. They direct the interest of the consumer to important points.

**3. Slogans:**

A slogan is a very single word or a group of words regularly used by the advertiser to impress upon the readers a basic idea about the product.

E.g.: "MODELLA makes the Suit: Suit Malas you"

Cell One – Connecting India

Nokia - Connecting People

Bajaj – You can't beat a bajaj

Speed Post – One India One Rate

**4. Illustrations:**

These consist of photographs drawings, graphs, charts, paintings and other pictorial devices. The main idea behind giving illustration is to gain attention, comprehension, attitude change and behaviour change.

**5. Text or Body of the Copy:**

It conveys the story in detail from the selling point of view. The text is the written or spoken part of the advertisement that appears below the headline and sub headlines.

The text copy must include proof of claims to enhance conviction. It may form:

(*i*) Descriptions of how product works or is made.

(*ii*) Test results

(*iii*) Performance case histories
(*iv*) Testimonials or quotations from experts and
(*v*) Sales records and guarantees.

**6. Closing Idea :**

All efforts made so as to establish product awareness, knowledge, liking preference and conviction are designed with the sole purpose to persuade the reader to purchase the product.

**7. Identifications Mark:**

It is the advertiser's name brand name or identification mark or trade mark. A brand name, a symbol, a word, or a letter or a combination of two may be used as a means of communication that brings about an identity of the producer or a dealer.

All these elements or components of an advertisement copy should be well knit into a harmonious and symmetrical form.

## REVIEW QUESTIONS:

1. What is creativity?
2. What are the qualities of a good advertisement copy?
3. Explain the term "Sentimental Value"
4. What are the contents of an advertising copy
5. What are the components of an advertisement copy?

# 32 ADVERTISEMENT LAYOUT

## DESIGNING AND LAYOUT

Both carry the same meaning layout means arrangement of various components of the copy (i.e) heading sub heading, illustration, slogan etc., In the T.V. Commercials layout is known as story board which is a series of picture coinciding with the audio and scripts

## FUNCTIONS OF LAYOUT

### 1. Assembling Different Parts :

The main function of layout is to assemble and arrange the different parts or elements of an advertisement illustration, headline, sub–headlines, slogans, body text and the identification mark etc., and border and other graphic materials – into a united presentation of the sales message.

### 2. Opportunity of Modifications:

The layout offers an opportunity to the creative team's agency management and the advertiser to suggest modification before its approval and actual construction and production begins.

### 3. Specification for costs:

The layout provides specification for estimating costs, and it is a guide for engravers, typographers and other craft workers to follow in producing the advertisement.

## PRINCIPLES OF DESIGN AND LAYOUT OR ELEMENTS OF DESIGN AND LAYOUT

**1. Balance:**Balance is the law of nature. The reference point is the optical center of the advertisement. The weight of a layout element is affected by both size and intensity of colour and tone. Two units have the same weight and both the colour value and the size are equal. A small element may be equal in weight to a larger one lighter tone or less intense value.

**2. Proportion:** Proportion is closely related to balance, since it refers to the division of space among layout elements for pleasing optical effects.

**3. Contrast and Emphasis:**Contrast means variety. It gives life to the whole composition and adds emphasis to selected important elements. Advertisers always look to advertisements from completion point of view and desire the policy of the most important elements to attract the attention of the people.

**4. Eye – movement:**Eye –movement is the design principle which helps more. The eyes of the readers from element to element in the order given in the hierarchy of effects model for effective communication of the message in advertising.

**5. Unity or Harmony:** Unity or Harmony is another important design principle. Although each element should be considered as a separate unit in striving for balance, proportion, contrast and eye movement, the complete layout or design should appear as a unified composition.

## REVIEW QUESTIONS :

1. What is an advertisement layout?
2. Discuss the functions of layout
3. What are the principles of layout?

# 33 ADVERTISEMENT MEDIA

### What is Media?

Advertising media is a device that carries the message of the target consumers. Advertiser or producer always keeps himself in touch with the existing and prospective customs only through a medium. It is the responsibility of the advertiser to select a right type of media keeping in mind

1. The number of target consumers
2. Attractiveness of the copy and
3. Expensiveness.

### Media of Advertising :

There are various forms of publicity or advertising media. They are :-

A. Print Media – (i) Newspapers
(ii) Magazines and Journals.

B. Broad cast Media – (i) Radio
(ii) Television.

C. Out door Media

D. Direct Mail Media

E. Miscellaneous Media

**(A). Print Media**

(i) News papers:

**Advantages :-**
1. Low cost per Reader.
2. Flexibility.
3. Choice of Market.
4. Repetitive value.
5. Quite Response.

**Disadvantages :-**
1. Art work not displayed
2. Short life
3. Advertisement may be missed to be read by the audience.
4. Limited number of customers.

**(ii) Magazines and Journals:**

**Advantages :-**
1. Longer Life
2. Better reproduction

3. Specialized groups of readers.
4. Large number of Subscribers
5. Publicity of firm's name.

**Limitations:**

1. Inflexibility
2. High cost
3. Waste circulation
4. Limited circulation because of limited readers.
5. Not suitable for small advertisers – producers of new product – advertisers requires immediate appearance of advertisement.

## OUT DOOR ADVERTISING MEDIA

**Kinds :-**

1. Mural Advertising – advertising on walls by painting or pasting posters.
2. Advertising Boards – Fixed especially at points where people frequently keep assembling or moving.
3. Vehicular Advertising – Displayed in Vehicules
4. Electronic displays – or neon signs
5. Sky writing
6. Sandwich man.

**Advantages :-**

1. More Attention
2. Communicating quick and simple ideas of repetition.
3. Greater Coverage.
4. Most attractive
5. Introduction of new product easier.
6. Economical.
7. Offer greater selectivity.
8. It is semi – permanent.
9. Good medium to stress upon brand names and package identity.

**Disadvantages:-**

1. Brevity of message
2. Public adverse reaction
3. Has only presenting value.

## Direct Mail Advertising

It is advertising by mail where messages are sent direct to the customers. The various methods of direct mail advertising are leaflets, Sales letters, folders, booklets, catalogue, Brochers. There are 3 main steps in this type of advertising.

1. Preparing mailing list of persons to whom messages are to be sent.
2. Preparing advertising messages in an attractive manner and
3. Conveying the message to persons concerned.

**Merits:-**

1. Selectivity.
2. Flexibility.
3. Personal Contact.
4. Secrecy.
5. Elaborate Explanation of Product qualities.
6. Greater coverage.
7. Interest arousing
8. Lower Cost.

**Limitations:-**

1. Costly.
2. Preparation of mailing list is difficult.
3. Not suitable for mass consumption goods.
4. Lack of prestige.

## RADIO AND TV

**(a) Radio:** - It is a word of mouth advertising on a whole scales. It makes appeal to ears and not to eyes.

**Merits :**

1. Human touch in appeal
2. Variety of programmes
3. Messages at home
4. Little efforts on the part of listeners
5. Flexible and timely
6. Messages to Message
7. Economic

**Demerits :**

1. Perish ability of Message
2. No pictorial presentation.
3. High cost of time and talent
4. Selective medium
5. Repetition.
6. Unsuitable to certain products

**(a) Television:**It is more popular in U.S.A. It is a powerful audio visual medium and offers very great Possibilities from the point of view of the advertiser.

**Merits: -**

1. All merits of radio advertising
2. It adds to prestige.
3. More attractive and impressive message
4. Presentation through pictures.
5. Most advantageous to those advertisers whose products and services require demonstration.

**Demerits:-**

1. Costly offer
2. Limited range of T.V. viewers
3. Limited messages due to high cost.
4. High cost of television commercial production
5. Short lived.

## OTHER MEDIA

### 1. Film Advertising:-

There are three kinds of moving pictures

(i) Documentary

(ii) Advertising film

(iii) Sponsored Advertising film.

**Merits:-**

1. Wide Coverage.
2. Appeal to all sections of people
3. Advertiser can explain and demonstrate.

**Demerits:-**

1. High production cost.
2. Censorship.
3. Only to people who came to theatre.
4. Audience feel bore.

### 2. Promotional Advertising

**(a) Point of Purchase Advertising:-**

(i) Neon signs. (ii) Window display. (iii) Counter display. (iv) Wall Display (v) Special displays and shows. (vi) Show rooms. (vii) Exhibitions and trade fairs.

**(b) Trade Shows:-**

c) Samples, Coupons, and Premiums:-

d) Trading Stamps:-

### 3. Speciality Advertising:-

It means where advertiser presents some articles, free of cost to the existing and prospective customers. Such articles bear the name and address of the advertiser. This medium is low in cost having a repetitive value, consumer come to contact to the message very frequently.

## FACTORS INFLUENCING SELECTION OF MEDIA

1. The number of people influenced.
2. The class of people influenced.
3. Circulation or coverage of media.
4. Conditions under which people are influenced.
5. Nature of message.

6. Extent of competition.
7. Cost of Media.
8. Size and nature of the business.

Point of Purchase Advertising:-

This advertising is either by the manufacturer or through his dealer near to the place where products are sold. This is a direct method of advertising.

**Types:-**

1. Window displays.
2. Show rooms.
3. Exhibition.
4. Counter displays.

## REVIEW QUESTIONS

1. What is media?
2. What are the forms of media advertising?
3. What are the merits and demerits of print media?
4. List out the kinds of out door advertising media.
5. What are the merits and demerits of television and radio advertising?
6. What are the factors influencing selection of media?
7. What is point of purchase?

# 34 ADVERTISING AGENCY

## ADVERTISING AGENCY

It is a facilitating institution of the advertising industry. It helps the advertiser in the creation and production of advertising. These advertising agencies provides a full range of services to advertisers, from the conception of idea to the exposure of printing of an advertisement and therefore large advertising agencies organize various activities and maintain a formal structural relationship between various departments.

Some large industries organize their own advertising or publicity department to undertake the advertising task but sometimes they also take help from the agencies. More often they engage experts and specialists. But small-scale industries do not have any other option but to employ an advertising agency.

The advertising agency performs all the necessary functions on behalf of the customer or advertiser and therefore if an advertising agency is appointed at all the advertiser must co-operate with it. The advertiser must consider different factors before selecting an agency and must be very particular that it should not be changed very often.

There are three components of the advertising industry. They are

- Sponsor or Advertiser
- Media
- The advertising agency

### Organisation of an advertising agency:

Like other organizations, the organization of advertising agency shows the formal authority relationship. The major operational responsibilities may be as creative services, account management, research and promotional services. The structure may be arranged on departmental or group basis.

### Functional Departments of an Advertising Agency:

The various functional departments in an agency organization are:

1. *Control Department*:: To get new business and maintain the existing one
2. *Media Department*: To contact media and take media decisions
3. *Copy Department*: The department coordinates the work of copywriting with the assistance of copy chief and copywriters.
4. *Art and visualization department*: It is the duty of the department to get the visuals and layouts prepared for press advertisements: posters, calendars, painted bulletins, car cards and other outdoor pieces.
5. *Production Department*: When a copy is ready the agency proceeds to its mechanical production through its mechanical production department headed by a director

**ORGANISATION CHART OF AN ADVERTISING AGENCY**

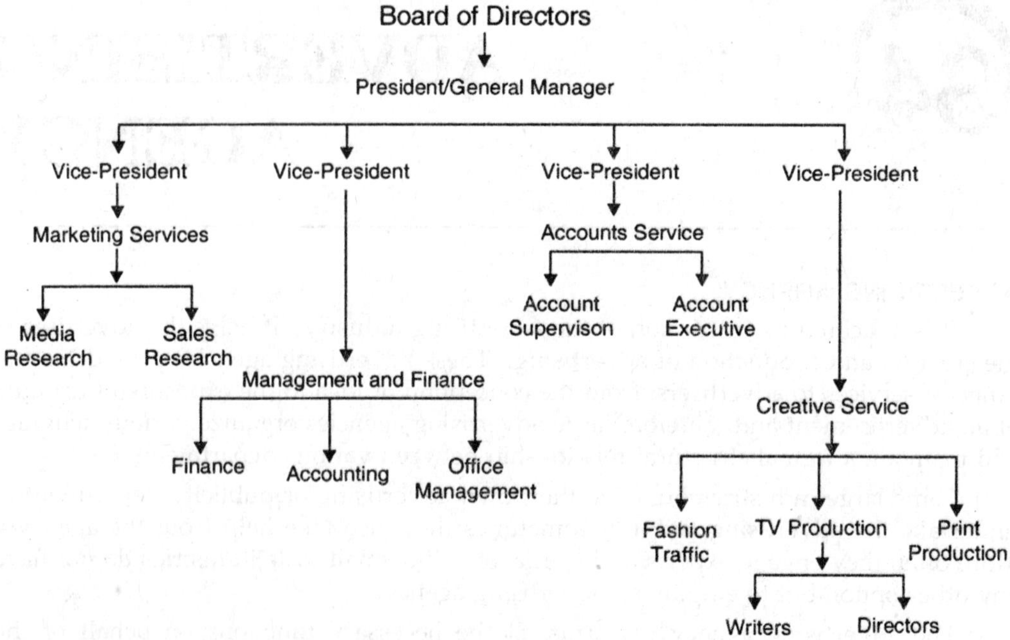


6. *Finance Department*: This department is responsible for maintaining accounts, billing and collecting the dues from its clients, verifying the appearance of advertisements.

7. *Research department*: This department of advertising agency is engaged in the study of the effects of sales activities at the last point of distribution of a particular product

8. *Public relations department* This department establishes and maintain mutual understanding between the organization and the public

**Main services Rendered by the advertising agency :**

- Timely and satisfactory work
- Boom to small and medium sized units
- Sound appropriation of funds
- Conducting market research
- Non advertising activities like designing products, determining prices etc.,

It is essential to use an Advertising Agency:

Big advertiser maintains their own advertising or publicity department under marketing department and takes full advertising activities. They do not employ advertising agency but instead employ various experts and specialists. In cases where this department does not perform full activities, the help of agency is taken. The small firms do not take the help of advertising agency.

**Major functions of Advertising Agency :**

- Selection of prospects
- Advertising planning by conducting extensive market research and media planning

- Media selection
- Creative function
- Research
- Marketing functions
- Co-ordination

## METHODS OF REMUNERATION

The main motive of all business is to earn profits and the business of advertising is not an exception to it. There are two popular methods for compensating advertising agencies for their services,

- Commission Method
- Fee Method or system

### 1. Commission Method of Compensation:

Under this system, the agency receives an amount equal to 15% of the cost charged for media space or time as the commission from media owners. The rate of commission varies from media to media and from country to country but 15% rate is almost universal.

The commission system has the sanction of long usage and is widely used because of its simplicity. This system simplifies the task of media greatly as the agency is directly concerned for the payment of media charges. The system also stimulates the productivity of agencies due to keen compensation for accounts

### 2. Fee System:

Under this system, the agency payment would consist exclusively of services fees which were to be computed on the basis of cost plus system. Under the system a certain fixed percentage of cost may be charged as fee to be paid to the agency along with the bill.

## ADVANTAGES

- The fee enables the agency to make a fair profit on services rendered by it and, in turn, the advertiser pay for what he gets – nothing more and nothing less.
- Most of clients paying under fee system, feel that agency is more objective in its recommendations,
- The agency is induced to provide a number of services, not tenable under commission system, if asked by the client because it will get more fee
- The agency's is income is stablised. Unforeseen costs in advertising expenditure by the advertiser do not affect the agency profits because it will get a fixed fee for the services whether media owner charge more or less.

In 1980's a Third system of compensation called the ***"Incentive based compensation system"*** was initiated.

## SELECTING AN ADVERTISING AGENCY

The advertising agency plays a very important role in advertising. While selecting an advertising agency the importance of consistency should be borne in mind. The agency takes a very long time in understanding the problems and accumulating the facts that are necessary for the smooth functioning of an account.

Therefore, an agency should not be changed frequently, for that result in repeated wastage of investment period.

**1. Changing an advertising agency :**

- The agency should possess good experience
- The agency should be able to think independently
- The size of the agency should not be taken seriously
- The agency should follow the advertiser in every case
- The agency should be able to undertake the market research
- The advertiser should think that the agency makes a profit on the account
- The agency should be financially sound and have good contacts with media owners

**2. How to get best out of an agency:**

The next problem, after selection of an agency, is how to use it to the best of its ability. For this purpose, the advertiser should co-operate with the agency. He should take the following steps in this connection.

- The advertiser should provide all possible information
- The agency should be challenged to produce results
- The advertiser should go as far as possible to keep the agency on its talent
- The advertiser should not allow the agency personnel to contact the junior staff of the company
- The advertiser should not interfere in the working of the agency
- The agency should be paid extra for extra work
- The advertiser should examine the work his agency does, for other parties to get new ideas.

## TYPES OF AGENCY:

### A. Special Service Group :

Service groups perform specialized services such as advertising planning, media planning creativity etc., Planning, media planning creativity etc., Printers, photo engravers etc are examples of such specialized groups.

### B. In House Agency

It is a full service agency and performs all the activities relating to advertising.

### Role of measuring Advertising Effectiveness:

All advertising efforts are directed mainly towards the achievement of business, marketing and advertising objectives (i.e.) to increase the sales turnover and thus maximum profit. The advertiser spends lakhs of rupees in to this advertising activity. In the background of all these efforts, is an attempt to attract the customer towards the product through advertising

In order to measure the effectiveness of advertising copy, two types of tests – pretests and post tests can be undertaken.

Pretests are generally conducted in the beginning of the creation process and post tests at the end of creation process or production stage. There are several pre and posttests techniques to measure the effectiveness of the advertising copy.

The effectiveness of advertising in a particular media may also be measured in any, of the following ways-

(a) By giving different addresses to different media.

(b) Different newspapers may be selected for advertisements of different departments.

(c) Coupon blank etc, may be provided with the advertisement

(d) Enquiry from consumers should mention the name of the source of information. The technique is known as keying the advertising.

Thus in measuring the effectiveness of advertising we include measuring of the effectiveness of advertising campaign, advertising copy and the effectiveness of individual media.

## IMPORTANCE OF MEASURING THE EFFECTIVENESS OF ADVERTISING

### 1. To get the cost benefit of advertising

The cost of advertising is mounting day by day and consequently profits are being squeezed. So the top management should be concerned about the cost benefit of advertising in the various items of expenditure in the balance sheet of the company, the contribution of which cannot be measured in terms of sales or profitability.

The main concept is that additional cost of advertising must produce additional profit and therefore, the advertising should prove its contribution in total marketing efforts like any other allocation of corporate resources or else. The advertising expenditure will be set arbitrarily or be slashed drastically

The cost must be linked with the benefits derived. If contribution of any advertising campaign is higher, it means the cost benefit is higher and the advertisement is effective.

### 2. To justify the investment in Advertising:-

The expenditure on advertisements is considered to be an investment. In any investment decision planning, there is always a statement of objectives, which are spelt out in detail, together with the nature and size of the returns expected on investment.

In order to justify the investment in advertising, the management makes an attempt to measure the effectiveness of the advertisement

### 3. To compare the results, with the objectives and goals.

An objective is a broad aim; a goal is specific and quantified objective. The objective is not measurable where as the goal is Generally the objectives of advertising are warded vaguely in general terms such as to increase sales or profits or to expand our share of market or to maintain a favourable attitude of the company and its product

The results are (actual sales) compared with the goods and if the actual performance is better, the advertising is effective otherwise, it is ineffective

### 4. To know the communication effect

The effectiveness of the advertisements can be measured in terms of their communication effects on the target consumers or audience. The main purpose of advertising is communicated to general public and existing and prospective consumers, various information about the product and the company. If the advertisements succeed in communicating the desired information and develop the favourable attitude, the advertising is effective.

**5. Compare two markets:**

Advertisers frequently seek to evaluate alternative types and amounts of advertising by experimentation in so called test markets. Under this procedure, advertising is published in test markets and results are contrasted with other markets – so called control markets – which have had the regular advertising programme. The measurements made to determine results may be measurements of change in sales, change in consumer attitudes, changes in dealer display, and so on depending upon the objective sought by the advertiser.

**6. Basis for planning:**

Measuring the effectiveness of the advertising is done with a view to improve the advertising plan by having a comparative view of the objectives set out in the plan and the objectives or goals achieved during the course of execution of the plan.

**How can advertising manager evaluate the effectiveness of a firm's advertising?**

Advertising is aimed at improving the sales volume of a concern, so its effectiveness can be evaluated by its impact on sales. Most of the managers believe that the advertisement directly affects the sales volume and hence they evaluate the effectiveness of the advertising campaign by the increase in the sales volume.

There may be two types of measures:

1. Direct measures and
2. Indirect measures

**Direct measures of advertising Effectiveness:**

**(a) Historical sales method:**

The historical sales analysis method is only a post test measure of advertising effectiveness and is not applicable to pre testing. It means that in this analysis, advertising effectiveness can be measured only when sales are effected and not earlier.

**(b) Experimental Control:**

This method is quite expensive when related to other advertising effectiveness measures. Yet it is possible to isolate advertising contribution to sales.

**(*i*) Before and after with control group design :**

This classic design uses several test and control cities. In this design two types of cities are selected. Cities in which advertising campaigns are affected may be named as test cities and other cities may be called central cities.

The normal sales level is calculated for both types of cities prior to advertising campaign, and then the advertising campaign is presented to the test cities and not the central cities. The effect of advertising campaign can then be measured by subtracting the amount of post campaign figure of sale from the pre campaign sale figures in test cities.

**(*ii*) Multivariable experimental designs:**

Multivariable designs produce these explanations and are, therefore, used by some very large firms because of their diagnostic value.

**2. Indirect measures**

As it is very difficult to measure the direct effect of advertising on company's profits or sales, most firms rely heavily on indirect measures.

The assumption of these measures is that favourable change in customer awareness, attitude and recall will lead in some way or the other to the attainment of greater sales and profits or whatever is the primary object of the marketing and corporate strategy.

The most commonly used measures are:-

1. Exposure to advertisement
2. Attention or recall of advertising message content
3. Brand awareness
4. Comprehension (obtaining information about the product
5. Attitude change
6. Action

## REVIEW QUESTIONS

1. Define – Advertising Agency
2. What is a organisation of an advertising agency?
3. List out the functional departments of an advertising agency.
4. Discuss the services rendered by the advertising agency.
5. What are the major functions of an advertising agency?
6. Which methods of remuneration are followed by the advertising agencies?
7. How to select an advertising agency?
8. What are the types of advertising agency?
9. Discuss the role of measuring advertising effectiveness through advertising agency.
10. What is the importance of measuring the effectiveness of advertising?

# Additional Questions

## SECTION A

1. Define Advertising
2. What is mass communication?
3. What is Advertising Budget?
4. What are Advertising Agencies?
5. What is Advertising Copy?
6. What is sampling?
7. Write the components of promotion mix?
8. What is personal selling?
9. What is advertising coverage?
10. What are sales?
11. What is a brand recall
12. What is the principle of canned presentation?
13. How does advertisement appeal help in purchase?
14. What are the constituents of advertisement budget?
15. What is the need for reminder advertisement
16. What is a corporate advertising?
17. Who is interested in a push strategy adapted by companies?
18. When does aggressive selling help the company?
19. How is the promotional efforts of company measured
20. How does premium attract customers?
21. Point out the nature of advertising
22. State any one advantage of advertisement in dailies
23. Mention any one objective of advertisement
24. What is meant by advertising budget?
25. Point of purchase advertising – Elucidate
26. Creativity in advertising – Comment
27. Who are the two parties linked by advertising agency?
28. From whom the advertising agent gets commission?
29. By which means, the effectiveness of advertisement could be sensed?
30. What is dust bin analysis?
31. Define sales management?

32. What is sales quota
33. State any two advantages of commission plan
34. What do you understand by Fringe benefit?
35. Who is a wholesaler?
36. Write a note on House to House selling
37. What is sales tax?
38. Explain the term sales turnover?
39. What do you mean by private warehousing?
40. What do you mean by supply chain management?
41. Define advertising
42. Define salesmanship
43. Describe advertisement copy
44. Explain advertising mix
45. State any four types of measure used for measuring effectiveness of advertising
46. What is an advertising agency
47. What are the objectives of sales promotion
48. What is meant be direct consumer offer?
49. Discuss Sales force promotions.
50. Explain personal selling.
51. What do you mean by recruitment of sales force?
52. What are the main objectives of Training?
53. Denote methods of compensation.
54. Specify reasons for a good remuneration plan
55. Define Channels of Distribution
56. What do you mean by wholesaler?
57. What is sales management
58. Write a short note on Sales Tax
59. What is warehouse receipt
60. What is meant by warehouse

## SECTION B

1. Explain the importance of advertising
2. What are the components of communication process
3. What are the characteristics of advertising copy
4. Explain the essentials of good appeal
5. What are the functions of advertising agencies
6. What are the components of direct advertising?
7. Explain the objectives of sales promotion
8. List out the qualities of salesman

9. What are the objectives for promotional activities?
10. Distinguish sales promotion and advertising
11. Describe the objective of advertising as an element of marketing mix
12. Discuss about the process of communication in advertisement
13. Explain the advertising experience and their role in marketing
14. Examine the roles and responsibilities of advertising agency
15. What are the components of advertisement budget
16. How do you differentiate various advertisement appeals?
17. Critically evaluate various forms of sales promotion
18. How do you formulate aggressive selling strategies?
19. How do you distinguish sales promotion and personal selling?
20. How do you measure the effectiveness of company's promotion efforts?
21. Describe any two types of advertising
22. What is your view on glamour in advertisements?
23. Examine any two objectives of advertisements?
24. Indicate about advertisement expenditure outlay
25. Explain about the planning of advertisement?
26. What do you understand by window display method of advertisement?
27. Is an advertising agency required? Why?
28. On what basis, an advertising agency is compensated?
29. Indicate any two benefits of advertising
30. Comment on legal control on advertising
31. Describe the various types of sales quota
32. Examine the need for training of sales force
33. Discuss the requisites of a sound compensation plan
34. Explain the procedure for performance evaluation of sales force
35. State the function and services of a Retailer to Consumer
36. What are the functions of Distribution channels
37. Explain the procedure for Registration in detail under the TNGST Act.
38. What are the various legal aspects involved in Sales Management
39. What is Distribution Requirements Planning system? Explain its objectives
40. Under what circumstances in private warehousing a better choice? Explain
41. Briefly explain the communication process
42. What are the social responsibilities of advertising?
43. What is the role of slogan in advertising?
44. The size of the advertising appropriation should be based on advertising effectiveness" Comment
45. Is it absolutely essential to use an advertising agency?
46. What criteria should be used to measure the success of advertisements?
47. Differentiate between a push strategy and a pull strategy

48. Name and describe the important objectives of promotion for demand stimulation
49. Is the cost per message delivered the right basis for evaluating alternative promotion methods?
50. Explain the purpose of point of purchase promotion
51. What is advertising management? Discuss the major institutions in it.
52. Explain the scope of advertising
53. What are the factors that are considered in setting the advertising objectives?
54. Explain the various models of Advertising budgeting
55. What are the objectives of an advertising campaign?
56. What are the various steps in campaign planning?
57. Explain the main services of the advertising agency
58. Explain the procedure of selection of advertising agency
59. Explain the importance of measuring the effectiveness of advertising
60. What are the stages of consumer decision process?
61. State the objectives of advertising
62. What are the criticisms against advertising?
63. Explain the factors to be considered for the advertising copy policy
64. Describe the steps involved in the budgetary process
65. Discuss the chief methods of testing the effectiveness of a message
66. Explain the service activities performed by the advertising agencies
67. What are the internal factors responsible for sales promotion?
68. What are the limitations of sales promotion
69. What are the basic promotional tools used to strengthen the sales force promotion
70. How personal selling differs from advertising
71. Define advertising. What are the importance of advertising
72. What are the benefits of advertising
73. What are the ethical issues in advertising
74. Would the economy be better of without advertising? Explain
75. Write a note on Local advertising?
76. What do you understand by the term product life cycle?
77. What is copy writing?
78. Write a note on Direct Mail Advertising?
79. What are the objectives of pre testing?
80. What are the social issues in advertising?
81. Explain the objectives of sales management
82. Give the advantages of Training to salesman
83. What are the essentials of a good remuneration plan
84. Describe the qualities of sales force

85. What are the functions of marketing channel
86. Describe the characteristics of a dealer
87. Sales tax is an indirect tax – Discuss
88. Differentiate sales management and Personal selling
89. What are the essentials of a Good storage
90. What is Public warehouse? What are its advantages

## SECTION C

1. Explain the objectives of advertising
2. What are the steps followed in advertising planning process?
3. Explain the types of advertisement copy
4. What are the factors influencing the advertising budget
5. Explain role of advertising expenses
6. Explain the testing methods available for the determination of advertising effectiveness
7. What are the advantages and limitations of sales promotion?
8. Explain the process of personal selling
9. Explain the kinds of sales promotion
10. Explain the elements of advertisement copy.
11. How does advertising help salesman in promoting the sales of product and services?
12. Discuss about the scope of advertising and its growth in the industry
13. What are the key guidelines of copy writing in advertisements?
14. Discuss about various forms of advertising in promoting products and services
15. Describe the formal organizational structure of an advertising agency
16. How do you measure the effectiveness of different advertising
17. What are the pre and post sales promotion activities in marketing of services?
18. List various sales promotional tools and its application in marketing
19. Multinational companies are professional selling to a maximum extent – Comment
20. "FMCG products have been extensively promoted by sales promotion techniques" – Discuss.
21. Examine the economic, social and ethical aspects of advertising
22. Evaluate the different advertising strategies so as to attract customers
23. Compare any two advertising media and explain their impact
24. As a manufacturer of a consumer product what are the factors you would evaluate while choosing an advertising agency?
25. List out the criticisms against modern advertisements and state the corrective measures thereof.
26. Explain the various methods of training in sales force

27. Briefly discuss the territory manager's problems
28. Explain the various methods of Remuneration of sales force
29. Identify and explain the determinants of sales force performance
30. Briefly discuss the function and services of a wholesaler to manufacturers
31. Discuss the important of distribution management in Modern Times
32. State the differences between Excise and Sales Tax
33. Discuss the functions and problems of Sales Tax in India
34. What are the various kinds of warehousing? Explain
35. Discuss the need of handling and storing equipments
36. Describe the objectives and functions of advertising
37. As an advertisement manager of a large firm how would you ensure a good relationship with your advertising
38. Explain the various methods of determining the advertising budget
39. Discuss the use of testimonials in advertising would they be suitable for all type of products?
40. Promotion is described as a process of communication between the seller and the buyer. In what ways significant to marketing does this communication process differ for personal selling and advertising?
41. Describe the types of promotional campaign that would probably be most appropriate and effective for (a) Chocolates (b) Car Batteries
42. Discuss the various functions of advertising
43. Explain the social responsibilities of advertising
44. How do you allocate the advertising budget?
45. Explain the factors that affecting consumer behaviour
46. What are the considerations in advertising agency selection?
47. Classify the advertising copy according to style
48. What are the major functions of an advertising agency?
49. Explain the types of agency organisation
50. What are the major responsibilities of an advertising department of a manufacturer?
51. How can an advertising manager evaluate the effectiveness of a firms advertising?
52. Explain the benefits of advertisement
53. Explain the advertisement in the marketing
54. Explain the factors that influencing the advertisement budget
55. Describe the different kinds of advertisement copies
56. Explain the essential guidelines for advertising measurement
57. Discuss the functions of advertising agency
58. Explain the tools used for sales promotion
59. Explain the advantages of sales promotion

60. Explain the advantages of personal selling
61. Explain how the effectiveness of promotion of a company can be measured.
62. What is newspaper advertising? Briefly explain the advantages of Newspaper advertising.
63. What are the special merits of Television advertising?
64. What is out door media advertising? What are the advantages and limitations of outdoor media advertising?
65. What are the essentials of an advertisement appeal?
66. What is advertising budget? What are the various advertising budgeting?
67. What are the controversial effects of advertising?
68. What are the factors to be considered in setting advertising objectives?
69. What are the internal and external factors which influence advertising efforts?
70. What are the areas of assessment of advertising effectiveness?
71. What resources are available to small retailers who cannot operate their own advertising departments economically?
72. Explain the importance of Sales organisation
73. Describe 'training programme'
74. Explain the various methods of compensation of sales force
75. Discuss the importance of right selection of sales force
76. Explain the types of channels of distribution
77. Explain the functions of retailers
78. Write short notes on TNGST, CST
79. "Sales executives is as co-coordinator" Discuss.
80. Explain the advantages and disadvantages of warehouse
81. Explain the advantages and disadvantages of storage.

## SALES AND DISTRIBUTION MANAGEMENT

1. What do you mean by recruitment of sales force?
2. What are the main objectives of Training?
3. Denote methods of compensation
4. Specify reasons for a good remuneration plan
5. Define 'Channels of Distribution'
6. What do you mean by "Wholesaler"?
7. What is sales management?
8. Write a short note on "Sales Tax"
9. What is warehouse receipt?
10. What is meant by warehouse?
11. Explain the objectives of Sales Management
12. Give the advantages of Training to Salesman
13. What are the essentials of a good Remuneration Plan?
14. Describe the qualities of Sales force
15. What are the functions of marketing channel?
16. Describe the characteristics of a dealer
17. Sales Tax is an Indirect Tax – Discuss.
18. Differentiate Sales Management and Personal Selling
19. What are the essentials of a Good Storage?
20. What is Public Warehouse? What are its advantages?
21. Explain the importance of Sales Organisation
22. Describe the Training Programme
23. Explain the various methods of compensation of sales force
24. Discuss the importance of Right Selection of Sales Force
25. Explain the types of channels of Distribution
26. Explain the functions of Retailers
27. Write short notes on: TNGST, CST
28. Sales Executive as coordinator. Discuss
29. Explain the advantages and disadvantages of wareshouse
30. Explain the advantages and disadvantages of storage.

## SALES AND ADVERTISING MANAGEMENT

***Give a short notes on the following:***

1. Sales planning
2. Sales Territories
3. Sales Policy
4. Selection of Sales force
5. Advertisement
6. Ethics in Advertising
7. Media Research
8. Advertising agencies
9. Cooperative advertising
10. Sachar Committee
11. What are the factors to be followed in the framing of sales policy?
12. What is Military type of sales organization? Explain its merits and demerits
13. What are the benefits of Marketing planning?
14. Mention the fundamental qualities required for a good salesman
15. What is Institutional advertising
16. Write a note on commercial advertising
17. Explain about Window Display
18. State the significance of News paper advertising
19. What are the advantages in using of an advertising agency?
20. How advertising Budget is prepared?
21. Discuss the importance of Sales Organization
22. What are the factors influencing the Marketing Management? Explain its goals
23. What are the sources available for the recruitment of Salesmen? Comment on each source
24. Explain the essentials of a good salesmen training programme
25. Explain the objects and importance of advertising
26. What are the objections against advertising?